W9-AUO-772

Presented to:

From:

Date:

Make Your Day Count
Devotional
for Teachers

Presented by

Lindsay Roberts and Friends

Harrison House
Tulsa, Oklahoma

Unless otherwise indicated, all Scripture quotations are taken from *The Holy Bible: New International Version*®
NIV ®. Copyright © 1973, 1978, 1984 by International Bible Society. Used by permission of Zondervan Publishing
House. All rights reserved.

Scripture quotations marked NKJV are taken from *The New King James Version*. Copyright © 1979, 1980, 1982,
Thomas Nelson, Inc.

Scripture quotations marked TLB are taken from *The Living Bible* © 1986. © 1971. Used by permission of Tyndale
House Publishers, Inc., Wheaton, Illinois 60189. All rights reserved.

Scripture quotations marked NCV are taken from *The Holy Bible, New Century Version*, copyright © 1987, 1988,
1991 by Word Publishing, Dallas, Texas 75039. All rights reserved.

Scripture quotations marked NLT are taken from the *Holy Bible, New Living Translation*, copyright © 1996. Used by
permission of Tyndale House Publishers, Inc., Wheaton, Illinois 60189. All rights reserved.

Scripture quotations marked THE MESSAGE are taken from *The Message: New Testament*, copyright © 1993 by Eugene
H. Peterson, published by NavPress, P.O. Box 35001, Colorado Springs, Colorado 80935. Used by permission.

Scripture quotations marked KJV are taken from the *King James Version* of the Bible.

Make Your Day Count Devotional for Teachers
ISBN 1-57794-660-X
Copyright © 2004 by Lindsay Roberts
Oral Roberts Ministries
Tulsa, OK 74171-0001

Published by Harrison House, Inc.
P.O. Box 35035
Tulsa, Oklahoma 74153

Manuscript compiled and edited by Betsy Williams of Williams Services, Inc., Tulsa, Oklahoma;
www.williams.services.inc@cox.net.

Printed in the United States of America. All rights reserved under International Copyright Law.
Contents and/or cover may not be reproduced in whole or in part in any form without the
express written consent of the Publisher.

Contents

Introduction

Chances are, you're like me—you lead a busy life with many demanding responsibilities. Your days are filled from sunup to sundown, and your to-do list is never-ending. But do your days always get off to a good start?

What we do first thing in the morning sets the tone for the rest of the day—both in our lives personally and, in your case, your classroom. The purpose of this book is to give you a bite-sized bit of godly wisdom each day so that you start out on the right foot, aware of God's presence in your life.

I have shared some things I have gleaned over the years in my walk with the Lord. And since no one knows the needs of teachers like teachers themselves, we've chocked this book full of insights and wisdom from others who share your profession. To wrap it up, after each devotion we've included an action step, something practical you can do each day to apply what you've learned.

Last but not least, you will find some helpful tips and quick-and-easy, mouth-watering recipes you are sure to enjoy. My goal, and that of the other contributors, is to help you start each day out right and *make your day count!*

Blessings,
Lindsay

Someone to Watch over You

Lindsay Roberts

Lead me in thy truth, and teach me: for thou art the God
of my salvation; on thee do I wait all the day.
—Psalm 25:5 KJV

We all need someone to watch over us and lead us in the right direction from time to time. For me, one of those people has always been my mother.

I was only twelve years old when my father died of cancer. My mother raised my brother, my sister, and me by herself in the turbulent sixties. I watched her not just talk about God's Word, but live its truths every day. And because she did, we constantly saw miracles in our household and came to know that God is real.

Mother walked around talking to God as though He was right in the room. My friends would ask, "Who's she talking to?"

I'd answer, "She's talking to the Lord," as if it was the most natural thing in the world.

When my brother, sister, or I asked for permission to do things, she always said, "I'll pray about it." That meant, "Not until I feel that God says it's okay." We had to go through Mom and God to get permission to do anything! But that's how God became real to us, and today we're all living for Him.

I'm sure that being a teacher isn't always easy, but the good news is, you are never alone. Your heavenly Father is always there, always watching over you, always helping you to be the best teacher you can be. Let Him help you today.[1]

make **your** day count

As you become aware of your students' needs, let them know you are praying for them. If you are teaching in a Christian school, offer to pray with them at those very moments, reminding them that when they pray according to God's promises, He always answers.

Undivided Attention

June Anne Wakley

Lord, hear my voice!
Let Your ears be attentive
To the voice of my supplications.
—Psalm 130:2 NKJV

"Teacher! Teacher! Teacher!" There she sat with her hand raised, calling out for my attention, right in the middle of my language arts lesson.

"Not now, Emily," I would respond to these frequent interruptions. I knew her comments were not about our lesson, but rather about something she wanted to tell me from the night before.

Every day Emily seemed to pick the worst time to remember something that she felt was of extreme urgency. She "needed" to tell me or she would not be able to concentrate for the remainder of the lesson. I had to find a way to give Emily the attention she needed and also teach the rest of my students without interruption. I began asking God to show me how I could resolve this situation. Then one day, I got it!

The next morning I had papers waiting on every student's desk, which they could begin working on independently. As they got started, I called Emily over to my desk and allowed her time to tell me all about the previous evening. In about two minutes, she was done and returned to her seat. And she didn't interrupt any lesson that day! From this I learned that if I would give Emily two minutes of my undivided attention, she would give me a full day of hers.

Isn't God wonderful to give us creative ideas so that everyone wins! And even more importantly, aren't you glad we always have God's undivided attention! The heavenly Father is never too busy for you. Spend some time with Him today, and tell Him all about everything.

make **your** day count

Be attentive to the voice of your students' supplications as well as to their unspoken needs today. Often you can tell by a student's body language that he or she is hurting or in need. Ask God to reveal your part in meeting that need.

Making a Difference

Amanda Pilgrim

"You are the world's light—a city on a hill, glowing in the night for all to see. Don't hide your light! Let it shine for all; let your good deeds glow."

—Matthew 5:14–16 TLB

Nicholas was a beautiful child inside and out, always full of eagerness and wonder, his little hands always forming some special project. Although he suffered from Muscular Dystrophy, Nicholas never let that hold him back. I never thought as I observed this little boy so full of excitement, that a year later I would be standing by his coffin consoling his mother.

After the service, his mother told me what an impact I had made in Nicholas' life, that he loved my class and thought I was "so funny," that he looked forward to seeing me and having me joke with him. I watched Nicholas fight many courageous battles due to MD, but it never occurred to me that I had made such an impression on him.

Every teacher dreams of making a difference in the lives of their students, but to have a grieving mother with tears in her eyes look at me and thank me for inspiring her child, for that I was not prepared.

I learned to look at life differently that day. I learned that a simple pat on the back or the few moments it takes to listen to the concerns of a child can make all the difference in the world. You never know how God will use you to bless and reach others.

make **your** day count

Take a moment to thank God for giving you an opportunity to bring joy to your students today. Give them a priceless gift—the gift of your smile.

time **saving** tips

Recharging Your Batteries

Try one these for a quick fix to get you through the rest of the day.

 Have a cup of specialty coffee or your favorite
soft drink.

 Play some fun music and sing along.

 Read something motivational from one of your
favorite authors.

 Step outside and get a quick breath of fresh air. Breathe
deeply and take in the beauty of God's creation.

 If it's not your day for lunch duty, find a quiet place
and take a quick power nap.

easy **recipes**

Lindsay's Frozen Grapes[2]

Wash grapes. While they are still wet, roll them in white sugar or a natural sugar substitute.

Place toothpick straight up in each one. Freeze and serve frozen.

Be aware that grapes are high in sugar. It's a natural fruit sugar, but it's still sugar.

My girls love to eat these frozen grapes. You can serve them frozen in chicken salad or fresh lettuce salads. The grapes thaw quickly and add a cold twist to your salads.

Recipe for a Happy Student

Karen Hardin

If any of you lacks wisdom, he should ask God,
who gives generously to all without finding fault,
and it will be given to him.

—James 1:5

Avoiding eye contact, my eight-year-old pretended to work on the lesson before him. Thirty minutes had elapsed, yet the paper was almost blank.

"Michael, you can do this!" I urged, almost pleading with my home-schooled son.

Math had been one of Michael's favorite subjects. But now his assignments were met with groans, delays, even tears. Searching for a clue as to his new attitude, I gained no insight other than the realization that he was beginning to *hate* math. "Give me wisdom, Lord," I prayed.

The next morning, Michael sat down for class. "Where's the math sheet?" he questioned.

"You don't have one today."

Michael's smile was quickly replaced by a suspicious look. "Why not?" he asked.

"We're going to make cookies instead."

Surrounded by measuring utensils, Michael added, subtracted, and worked on fractions as we calculated the ingredients for the recipe. The next day we prepared a bank deposit and counted coins. Another day we went to the grocery store with a list of items and a twenty-dollar budget. He loved it.

For the next few weeks, we didn't just do math, we lived it. When we did return to the traditional math sheets, I made sure that we interspersed them with occasional hands-on lessons. Math may not be Michael's favorite subject, but he doesn't hate it and now promptly completes his lessons.

make **your** day count

Students can learn in a variety of ways.
Ask God for wisdom as you plan today's lessons,
asking Him for creative applications that help make learning fun.

Responding vs. Reacting

Dana Hicks

A patient man has great understanding,
but a quick-tempered man displays folly.
—Proverbs 14:29

As a teacher of young children, I have to guard against "reacting" instead of "responding" to classroom situations daily. This year has been my most challenging yet in this area. As I read the above verse recently, it became apparent that I didn't have enough understanding and that was why I was letting some of the classroom situations control me rather than me controlling them.

I sensed the Holy Spirit prompting me to look up definitions for the words *react* and *respond*. The *American Heritage Dictionary, New College Edition* defines *react* as meaning, "to *act* in response or in *opposition* to some former act or state...to be *affected* or influenced by circumstances or events."[3] That was it! I was allowing myself to be affected by things and acting in opposition to the circumstances—and I did *not* like it!

Next I found that *respond* means, "to make a reply, to answer, to *react positively* or *cooperatively*."[4] I wanted to respond positively, in an assertive and helpful manner that I would feel good about. But *how?* Proverbs 17:27 states, "A man of *knowledge* uses words with restraint, and a man of *understanding* is even-tempered" (emphasis mine). The knowledge I needed was in 1 Corinthians 13—specifically verses 4–8—often referred to as the love chapter. The understanding I needed was to predetermine how I was going to respond to certain situations. When I did these things, I began to see tremendous changes in the children and me.

What made the change occur? It was understanding the difference between *responding* versus *reacting* and predetermining how I was going to handle situations before they occurred. I believe that as you put these principles into practice, you will experience positive changes as well.

make **your** day count

Think of a classroom scenario that you feel you handled poorly. Ask the Holy Spirit to help you predetermine how you should handle this situation in the future. God will help you as you begin to respond in the spirit of love instead of reacting in opposition.

time **saving** tips

Easing a Difficult Day

Inevitably you will be faced with a day that has been difficult and perhaps draining. Take a few moments to put aside the trials of the day and end it on a positive note.

Keep an inspirational book in your drawer:
Taking a few moments to read a passage in a book that inspires you can help to change the mood of the day.

Listen to a book on tape:
Use the commute home to listen to a tape or CD of that book you've been wanting to read.

Call a friend who makes you laugh:
Laughter is the best medicine to help you out of a slump. Find a way to make yourself laugh—it will lift your spirit and renew your strength.

Take a bubble bath:
Slip into a steaming bath with lots of bubbles and let your cares float away.

easy **recipes**

Claydough

Karen Hardin

This alternative for modeling clay is great for making crafts and decorations.

1 ³/₄ cups plain white flour
2 Tbsp. salt
¹/₂ cup cold water

Put the flour and salt in a large bowl.

Slowly add the water, mixing thoroughly.

Knead into a soft ball.

Use right away or keep in an airtight container or plastic bag.

When ready to use:

Preheat oven to 100°.

On a lightly floured flat surface, roll out claydough to approximately ¹/₄ inch thick.

You can use cookie cutters or come up with your own shapes that can be used as ornaments or any number of other craft ideas. Be creative!

Bake for 2–3 hours.

When cool, the pieces can be painted or decorated with felt-tip pens.

When color is dry, seal with varnish.

time **saving** tips

More Ways to Ease a Difficult Day

On a particularly challenging day, you may need to do all of these. Remember, tomorrow is a new day. You owe it to yourself and your students to begin it refreshed, replenished, and ready to go.

Keep a folder with notes of appreciation:

Keep a folder handy containing the notes of appreciation you receive from your students, their parents, and faculty members. It can bring a smile to your face and warmth to your heart.

Take the scenic route home:

It may take a little longer, but you will have the opportunity to appreciate the glory and beauty of God's creation.

Treat yourself:

Stop by the store and buy yourself a flower, a fun new soft drink, an aromatic candle, or that new outfit you've had your eye on. It's okay to reward yourself for a job well done.

Get or even give a hug:

Nothing feels better or is more comforting than the warmth of a hug from someone who cares. Even if you have to initiate it, give someone a hug. You're sure to get one in return.

Ziploc® Ice Cream[5]

This is a cute idea that can be done with the students in your classroom.

½ cup milk (any kind: whole, 2%, or chocolate)
1 Tbsp. sugar
¼ tsp. vanilla
Pint-size Ziploc® freezer bags
Quart or larger Ziploc® freezer bags
Ice
6 Tbsp. rock or regular salt

Add first three ingredients to a pint-size Ziploc® bag and zip shut.

Place that bag inside a larger, quart- or gallon-size Ziploc® bag.

Add ice to fill bag halfway plus salt (rock or regular).

Zip larger bag shut, and shake, turn, toss, and mix the contents in the bag.

In about 5 to 10 minutes, you will have cold hands and yummy ice cream.

Be sure to get all the salt off the small bag before opening it.

Note: does not work well to double the recipe.

Clothe Yourself with Wisdom… You're Going to Need It

Karen Hardin

She speaks with wisdom,
and faithful instruction is on her tongue.
—Proverbs 31:26

"Get your books out, and let's begin the reading assignment," I announced to the twenty students seated in front of me. In unison the class obeyed, that is except for Donald.

Donald was a bright kid and usually made good grades on the days he put forth the effort. Today obviously wasn't one of those days. While I was still contemplating my options regarding his behavior, Mr. Lee—the vice principal—walked into the classroom to speak with me. As he spoke, I caught movement out of the corner of my eye. Donald had quietly slipped out of his chair and grabbed the broom in the back corner of the room. He was now conspicuously sweeping every inch of floor space in the room.

How obvious can you get? I thought to myself while still trying to focus on Mr. Lee, who continued to speak for a few more seconds, oblivious to the performance behind him. As he delivered his message, he turned to acknowledge the class before leaving. Donald was ready, busy as ever.

"Donald, what an outstanding student you are," Mr. Lee offered before the entire class. Donald lowered his head slightly and offered a rather humble, and I'm sure well-practiced, smile. In my mind, I could sense Mr. Lee making a mental note of Donald's "voluntary assistance" as he exited the room. However, once Mr. Lee was gone, Donald tossed the broom aside and returned to his chair, his work done for the day.

It was clear mine was just beginning.

make **your** day count

Take a moment to pray before you enter your classroom
today and clothe yourself with the wisdom of God.
It is yours for the taking. You're going to need it!

Tulip the Clown

Cleo Justus

A merry heart does good, like medicine.
—Proverbs 17:22 NKJV

Our mission team had gone to Publeto, in the high desert area of Mexico to bring spiritual and physical help and hope to this very deprived group of people. Among the mission team were doctors, dentists, an optical team, a pharmacy, and yes—a clown, named Tulip!

As people met with the medical staff, I began my role as Tulip, singing, making animal balloons, and telling Bible stories. Unfortunately, the only place available to me was a shaded area dividing lanes of traffic. The children sat in the shady area, and I stood in the street, moving for an occasional vehicle. We sang songs, I entertained, and at last I told a Bible story.

Noticing a large group of men gathering nearby, I began to feel a little apprehensive. But I stayed busy with the children, determined to keep a watchful eye. Then, as the growing group merged closer, I noticed that the men were attentively listening!

At the end of my story, the children lined up to receive their animal balloons and sweet treats. Meanwhile, one of the men who had been close by called out, "We want to know more about what the clown is saying."

That afternoon, several gave their hearts to God and received Spanish Bibles. One man, stating his eagerness for our return, offered his home for meetings. Two months later, we did return—to an established mission holding weekly services!

What an honor it was to have had a part in the transformation of that small community. You see, as children of God, we are all teachers. And though it seems unlikely at times, someone is watching, listening, and hungering for a touch from God.

make **your** day count

Be on the lookout for someone who could use a little encouragement today. Lend an ear; offer a gentle kindness. You never know when you might be a flicker of hope to a hungry heart searching for a touch from God.

time **saving** tips

Incentive for Academic Achievement

Amanda Pilgrim

Encourage your students to strive for higher academic marks by having small rewards available.

One idea you might like to try is to fill six plastic eggs with small, inexpensive items like stickers, erasers, and small wrapped candy. In one of the eggs, include a free homework pass. Whenever students score 100 percent on a test, they have the opportunity to choose one egg. Whoever chooses the egg with the free homework pass in it is exempt from one assignment in the class in which he or she received the egg.

For example, if the student scores 100 percent in spelling, then the pass is good for one assignment in spelling. The passes cannot be used for tests, quizzes, or review papers.

What student wouldn't want the egg with the home-work pass in it! It may provide just the right incentive to motivate those students who have been lax in their work.

Sour-Cream Potato Casserole

1 large package frozen hash browns
1 pint sour cream
3 cans potato soup
$\frac{1}{2}$ tsp. garlic salt
Cheddar cheese, shredded

Thaw hash browns completely.

Mix sour cream, soup, and salt. Add potatoes.

Put into greased 9 x 13 inch casserole dish.

Top with cheese and bake for 1 hour at 350°.

Serves 10–12.

Setting an Example

Holly Sonnenschein

In everything set them an example by doing what is good.
In your teaching show integrity.

—Titus 2:7

Teachers set an example. Whether we realize it or not, our students are watching us, and everything we do makes an impression on them. Like thirsty sponges, they soak up everything we say or do.

In my own teaching experience, I have stood back and laughed as I have observed my students imitating me. For example, after school I once found a student holding a ruler, pointing to the board and teaching another student with the same mannerisms I use. Or, I've observed others dictating spelling words and having the class repeat after them as I do. Part of my teaching experience has taken place in Christian schools where we have chapel services, and I have noticed that during praise and worship times, the students raise their hands to worship when I do. When I clap, they clap with me.

If students see their teacher exhorting and encouraging, then they will do the same. If they see their teacher reaching out to help someone in need, they, too, will reach out. If they see their teacher excited about what he or she is doing, then they will get excited too.

Allowing the fruit of the Spirit to control our lives is one of the best examples we can set. Whether you have the liberty to talk openly about the things of God or not, your students will no doubt recognize the love, patience, and kindness you show them. They will see it when you use self-control when you should be going crazy! They'll notice the joy of the Lord working in your life, and they will want it too!

We can be a shining example of what we want our kids to be!

make **your** day count

Focus on one fruit of the Spirit today (Gal. 5:22–23), and purpose to allow that fruit to infuse all of your thoughts, all of your words, all of your actions. When you see that fruit mirrored by your students, openly acknowledge and encourage them.

Many Flavors

Linda Burritt

The body is not made up of one part but of many.
If the whole body were an eye, where would
the sense of hearing be? If the whole body
were an ear, where would the sense of smell be?
But in fact God has arranged the parts in the body,
every one of them, just as he wanted them to be.
You are the body of Christ, and each one of you is a part of it.
—1 Corinthians 12:14,17,18,27

Ever have one of those school years where there weren't enough corners for the students who needed separation from one another? One year was especially stressful for me with an entire classroom of challenging elementary students. I found myself eliminating fun projects and activities because certain students lacked self-control.

My frustration rose daily, and I was losing the joy of teaching. Even my morning prayer time had started to become lusterless and dry, until the Lord got my attention one morning.

As I was once again pointing out to God the many challenges and frustrations at school, I sensed Him gently say, *They're all mine, but they come in many flavors.* Wow! Many flavors—like ice cream! Had I lumped all my students under one heading like we do ice cream? Was I failing to see the individual variety and uniqueness of each child?

Yes, indeed I was. Repentance came quickly along with a new joy for the job and love for my individual students.

God's Word tells us that we are all wonderfully made in His image. All of nature declares His wondrous marvels and variety. I had been teaching that to my students, yet I had failed to deal uniquely with them. Frustrations stopped for them and for me as I began to respond to their "flavor" instead of the situation. Praise God for all our many "flavors."

make **your** day count

Make it a point to notice the different "flavors" your students represent today. For those particularly challenging students, endeavor to see the special characteristics that God has given them, those things that add to their individual uniqueness. Then build upon their strong points.

time **saving** tips

Creative Strategies for the Classroom

Linda Burritt

In math classes, starting the second semester, I set aside one day a week and pair up the students to play chess. It is an excellent way for them to develop their problem-solving skills.

I usually place the most difficult students near my desk so that I have more opportunities to develop relationships with them. I can quietly talk with them about things other than discipline issues. It allows me to give them more one-on-one attention and time for tutoring. I also have them run appropriate errands, which increases their sense of self-worth.

Speaking in a quieter voice helps with most discipline matters, I have found, and it helps the students learn self-control.

Every spring I start praying for my upcoming new class of students. That way I have more time to look to God for more creative ideas and activities, including preparation with the curriculum for the fall.

easy **recipes**

Fruit Pizza

A fun class project!

1 roll refrigerated sugar cookie dough
1 cup sugar
1 8-oz. cream cheese, softened
1 8-oz. Cool Whip®
1 small can crushed pineapple
1 or 2 kiwi, peeled and cut into thin slices
Fresh strawberries, cleaned, hulled, and thinly sliced
Bananas, sliced and dipped in lemon juice (to prevent browning)
Shredded coconut
Finely chopped pecans

Spread sugar cookie dough evenly on a pizza pan using fingertips.

Pierce a few times with fork tines and bake at temperature listed on package until lightly browned.

If it puffs up, press down slightly after you let it cool a little. Cool crust completely.

Beat softened cream cheese with sugar until smooth.

Fold in Cool Whip and blend thoroughly.

Spread this on the cooled crust.

Drain pineapple thoroughly and spread evenly over cream cheese mixture.

Arrange the slices of kiwi on top of the pineapple, then arrange the strawberry and banana slices.

Sprinkle with shredded coconut and chopped pecans.

Refrigerate until serving. Cut into pizza slices to serve.

time **saving** tips

Brighten the Day!

Georgia Lee Paul

It's a simple thing, but I have found that I get a more positive response from my students when I smile.

Pick a different student each day and do something kind especially for him or her. Start at the beginning of the alphabet and work your way through. It will do wonders for your students.

Greet your students at the door as they enter the class room, each with a positive observation or comment. Be as specific as possible.

easy **recipes**

Crock-Pot® Roast Beef

2–3 carrots, scrubbed and sliced lengthwise (or whole if small)
2–2 ½ lb. rump roast or cut of choice
1 onion, quartered
3–4 potatoes, scrubbed and quartered
½ cup soy sauce (or Bragg Liquid Aminos*)
1 beef bouillon cube
1 bay leaf
3–4 peppercorns
1 tsp. dried thyme
1 tsp. garlic powder

Put carrots and roast into Crock-Pot®.

Wedge onion around sides of roast.

Potatoes go on top.

Combine all other ingredients and pour over roast and vegetables.

Add water till it nearly covers roast.

Cook on low for 7 hours or until very tender.

*Bragg Liquid Aminos is an all-natural seasoning made from soy protein that tastes very similar to soy sauce. It has a small amount of naturally occurring sodium, but no table salt is added. It is available at most health food stores.

When Someone's Baggage Influences Your World

Lindsay Roberts

Let's please the other fellow, not ourselves, and do what
is for his good and thus build him up in the Lord.
—Romans 15:2 TLB

Most of us encounter at least one or two difficult people who seem to rip our peace right out from under us the minute they walk through the door. What do you do when that happens—especially when it's someone close to you?

The Bible tells us that God's love is the key. It's important to remember that the problem isn't the person who is trying to steal your peace. Ephesians 6:12 says, "Our struggle is not against flesh and blood, but against the rulers, against the authorities, against the powers of this dark world and against the spiritual forces of evil in the heavenly realms."

We all know good people with bad baggage. I believe that the spirit of fear is often behind the anxiety and torment people carry in their lives. When their baggage begins to influence your world, your responsibility is to be like God. God is love, so you are to demonstrate the love of God to them. You don't have to do this in your own strength, however. God's love has already been shed abroad in our hearts; we just have to yield to it and let it flow out of us. (Rom. 5:5.)

The next time someone's baggage begins to rub you the wrong way, remember: the love of God can remove that junk out of that person's life. And God will empower you to be patient and kind as you yield yourself to Him. Who knows, you may be just the one God wants to use to bring healing and wholeness to that person.[6]

make **your** day count

Seek out someone whose "baggage" is a challenge to you
and purposely bless the person with God's love today.

Dare to Dream

Karen Hardin

*Call to Me, and I will answer you, and show you great
and mighty things, which you do not know.*
—Jeremiah 33:3 NKJV

Standing in the classroom, I threw out the opening question for dialogue. "What would you do if you had a million dollars?" The question was simply an exercise to promote conversation in my class of nineteen Chinese university students, all studying English as a second language. The response was not what I had expected.

"I won't ever have a million dollars," replied the first pragmatically.

"What's the use of thinking about a million dollars?" stated another.

"Impossible," said the third.

My simple assignment, meant to promote conversational English, opened my eyes to the immense cultural differences we faced. Having grown up in America, I was always encouraged to dream. It never occurred to me that it was a privilege. We often take for granted that our Constitution guarantees our right to pursue happiness and the "American dream." In our culture, the impossible many times does become possible.

As a believer, I was also aware that I had been exposed to a truth that had never made its way into the ears of the majority of my students: "*Nothing* is impossible with God," (Luke 1:37, emphasis mine). Faith, hope, and dreams. They had not yet learned to dream. They didn't even know that they *could* dream or that God wanted to fulfill their dreams.

What are the dreams of your students? What potential do you see in them? As we invest in their lives—encouraging them to be the best that they can be, to know God and follow His plan for their lives—we are acting as a conduit through which God can lead them into a life that is beyond their wildest dreams.

make **your** day count

Talk to God today about the dreams in your own heart. Are they dreams that will bring glory to Him? As you encourage yourself in these truths, also encourage your students today. With God, *nothing* is impossible—for you or them!

Thank God for His Goodness and Mercy

Dana Hicks

Oh, give thanks to the LORD, for He is good! For His mercy endures forever. Let the redeemed of the LORD say so, whom He has redeemed from the hand of the enemy

—Psalm 107:1,2 NKJV

It is easy to praise God for His goodness when things are going our way. However, in the difficult times, we need to praise Him all the more! Even when life gets tough, God is still good and His mercy still endures forever; and we are to acknowledge it, say it, whisper it, shout it, sing it, and proclaim it any way we can!

As we read through Psalm 107, we are exhorted over and over again to give thanks to God for His goodness. If God is telling us to spruce up on thanking Him for His goodness, that tells me that He is at work, causing His goodness and mercy to shine through and overtake the difficult situations we face.

In Isaiah 55:11, God promises that His Word will accomplish the things for which it is sent. It's God's job to bring His promises to pass. We simply thank Him for His Word regarding our circumstances and for bringing His goodness and mercy to bear in them.

This year I have had the privilege of teaching a precious girl who has been diagnosed with Down's syndrome. According to all of the research, she should not be as successful in school as she has been. But since the day she was born, her parents have thanked God for His goodness and mercy concerning every area of her life. Today this girl is a living testimony of God's goodness at work, because she is doing the same curriculum as the rest of the class and doing it with a high degree of accuracy!

Never entertain thoughts that God is anything but good, but continually thank Him for His goodness. Then watch as He pours that goodness out on you!

make **your** day count

Think of a student, coworker, or friend who needs to see God's goodness and mercy penetrate his or her situation today. On that person's behalf, begin to thank God continually that His goodness and mercy will turn the difficult situation around. Then watch as God begins to move!

time **saving** tips

Lunch on the Go

Nourishing your body will provide much-needed energy to accomplish the many tasks you must perform each day. Try some of these ideas.

Prepare your meals the night before:

Pack a lunch, even something quick and light like a piece of fruit and some crackers. By doing this the night before, you will have one less thing to think about before hurrying out the door the next morning.

Keep a few packaged foods in your drawer:

Fruits like oranges and apples can stay fresh in a drawer for several days. Granola bars offer a nutritious alternative to that candy-filled vending machine and can give you a boost of energy. Even a package of instant oatmeal or soup in a coffee cup can be concealed while you rush off to your next engagement.

Keep extra change in your drawer for vending machines:

You never know when you might be working late or when you might have a sudden craving for a chocolate boost!

If possible have a small microwave and refrigerator in your room:

These small appliances will come in very handy. Not only are they helpful for storing or heating up a lunch on the go, but they are also highly beneficial for class projects.

Broccoli Casserole

Abby Detcher

1 bag frozen chopped broccoli
8 oz. Velveeta cheese, cubed
1 stick butter, cut into pieces
1 sleeve Ritz crackers, crushed

Cook broccoli in microwave according to directions, approximately 8 minutes.

Drain.

Top with cubed Velveeta, then Ritz crackers.

Put butter over cracker crumbs.

Bake at 350° for 30 minutes.

Loving Your Students

Emily Biffle

*Be gracious in your speech. The goal is to
bring out the best in others.*
—Colossians 4:6 MESSAGE

First and foremost, I believe that children need to feel acceptance and love in the classroom. When they feel safe, they are able to learn, make mistakes, and know they are still valued. Through us, they will experience the mercy and goodness of God, which will have a profound impact on them. When we as His children experience His grace in our lives, we feel we can open up to Him.

I've noticed that when I praise my students, it not only changes the attitude that they have toward themselves, but it also affects how I view them. One of the ways I like to do this is to stand at my door each morning and pat them on the back with an encouraging word as they enter the classroom.

I learned this from one of my professors in college who would stand near the door and welcome each student by name and even visit with his students before class. Of course, everyone loved Dr. Lashley, and there was always a waiting list to get into his class. We all felt connected to him, because he was connected to us.

Jesus was the ultimate teacher. He showed His love through so many ways, such as when He said, "Let the little children come to me" (Matt. 19:14). How blessed we are to have little children—and older ones—come to us every day.

make **your** day count

Stand at the door of your classroom this morning and greet your students by name, conveying your eagerness to spend the day with them.

time **saving** tips

Ideas for Bulletin Boards

Jackie Farell & Holly Sonnenschein

Designate one bulletin board in your room to a different student every few weeks. Put the student—and one of his or her parents—in charge of decorating the bulletin board with things about himself or herself. Pictures, cutouts, special award certificates and ribbons, and other creative objects that represent the student are welcome. Your class will find this very fun, and it will be one bulletin board you won't have to think about.

Dedicate a bulletin board to the students that they can use to "teach" one another about the things they are acquainted with. For instance, if a student loves horseback riding, he or she could decorate the bulletin board with all kinds of pictures and objects related to that hobby. A big baseball fan could put up favorite baseball cards, a hat with his or her favorite team's logo on it, and magazine articles and pictures about that team. Give the students a few minutes to introduce the class to their bulletin board, letting them share their knowledge with their classmates.

Showoff Shortbread

Lisa Anne Camille Louissaint

This is the yummiest cookie! It is impressive and easy! Definitely a crowd pleaser.

1 cup of softened butter (2 sticks)
½ cup granulated sugar
1 tsp. vanilla (Use white vanilla if you have it.)
2 cups all-purpose flour
2 pinches of salt (about ¼ tsp.)

Preheat oven to 300°.

Cream butter, sugar, and vanilla until fluffy.

Add flour and salt.

Spread and press into the bottom of a greased 9 x 13 inch pan (a little larger works well also).

Score into bars with a knife. Poke holes lightly with a fork.

Bake on middle rack for about 50 minutes. Cool on a rack, turn out of pan, and break on scored lines.

If you want to frost them, do so, but do not turn out. Lift out with a knife or small spatula instead.

Alternative:

Scoop out dough with a tablespoon and roll into balls.

Flatten slightly between palms.

Place 1 inch apart on an ungreased cookie sheet.

Bake at 350° for 15 minutes or until lightly browned.

Cool on baking sheet for one minute, then move to cooling rack.

time **saving** tips

Effective Bulletin Boards

Amanda Pilgrim

Don't be afraid to express yourself when it comes to your bulletin boards. Spice up your room by trying a different approach or look.

 Take pictures of the students and school activities and post them.

 Use wrapping paper, cloth, or lace for the background.

 Use it as a "message center" for your students.

Post assignments.

 Use 3-D items like cornstalks or toy spaceships to accent a theme.

 Color, color, color.

 Make your own cutouts using copies from a book or the computer. You can trace them onto the bulletin board with the help of an overhead projector.

 Use twisted brown butcher paper to make a vine-like border.

 Be creative and have fun!

A Cookie Gift

Purchase several quart-size canning jars, the kind with the ringed lids and round inserts. Get your favorite chocolate chip cookie recipe and layer all of the dry ingredients in the jar. First mix the flour, baking soda, and salt, and pour into the bottom of the jar. The next layer should be the brown sugar, then the white sugar on top of that. Finally, fill the remainder of the jar with chocolate chips.

Next, cut out seven-inch fabric squares, using pinking shears as a nice touch. If the gifts are for Christmas, use Christmas fabric, for instance. Place the round inserts on top of the jars, then center the fabric over them. Screw the rings on top of all.

On a small card, write out the remaining ingredients as well as the instructions for mixing and baking. Punch a hole in the upper left-hand corner of the card and attach it to the lid of the jar with ribbon, raffia, or elastic cording.

Celebrate Their Significance

Holly Sonnenschein

[Jesus said], "Look at the birds of the air; they do not sow
or reap or store away in barns, and yet your heavenly Father
feeds them. Are you not much more valuable than they?"
—Matthew 6:26

Every person alive longs to know that he or she is significant. Throughout God's Word, He tells us how much we are loved and that He has plans and purposes for our lives. He tells us that He even knows the number of hairs on our heads! He calls each star by name, and not even a sparrow falls to the ground without the Father knowing it.[7]

As teachers we can follow His example. We have the power to make our students feel special, to help them realize their potential, to help them see that there is no one quite like them.

I try to find out what I can about my students before we meet on the first day of school. I study their pictures from the previous year's yearbook, then I try to surprise them by calling them by name the first day they walk into class. Getting involved in their lives, attending their sporting events, and cheering them on are things I endeavor to do to show them I believe in them. Sometimes I call them at home to let them know what a blessing they are. They know that I am not only interested in their grades, but their lives and anything else that concerns them.

I believe that when we invest in our students in this way, we can have an impact upon their whole outlook on life!

make **your** day count

Call a student tonight and offer a word of encouragement about a specific way he or she has blessed your class. Ask if there are any concerns that you can be praying about, and offer to pray right then, if you feel it is appropriate.

A Substitute Teacher's Nightmare Come True

Jackie Farell

[Jesus said] "Be wise as serpents and harmless as doves."
—Matthew 10:16 NKJV

I walked into the physics class only to have the nightmare stories of being a substitute teacher become reality. It was my first day to substitute teach. I had heard stories about kids trying to take advantage of the teacher, but had hoped they were exaggerations. In my case they weren't.

When I asked the ninth graders to take their seats, one young man by the name of Eric simply ignored me and, with his back to me, kept talking to a small group of boys as if I weren't even there. When he finally did sit down, he kept making wisecracks and comments under his breath. Quickly I prayed and asked God to give me wisdom in the situation.

"Lord, your Word says, 'If any of you lacks wisdom, he should ask God, who gives generously to all without finding fault, and it will be given to him'" (James 1:5). I had hardly finished praying when I felt inspired of the Holy Spirit to use this situation to my advantage.

"Eric!" I began. "Since I am not as familiar with this classroom as you are, would you please be my assistant today and help me teach?"

After the shock wore off that I would even consider putting him in a position of leadership, Eric jumped up enthusiastically. I told him what physics experiments we were supposed to do, and he distributed all the equipment to each table and assisted me in any way I needed. From that point on, the class went very smoothly. The students seemed to enjoy their time with me, and to my surprise some even complimented me on being their favorite substitute. With God's help, any situation can be turned around!

make **your** day count

When you are faced with a situation and have no idea
what to do, send up an SOS to God and ask for His wisdom.
He sees the big picture and knows how to get things under control.
But don't just wait for a crisis. Call on God's wisdom all through your day.

time **saving** tips

Celebrating the Gifts and Strengths of Your Students

Encourage your students to share their gifts and talents to enhance the classroom environment and to help them develop their strong points.

Openly praise:

People who are praised openly tend to work harder and are more devoted to those who compliment them. This can build self-confidence and help minimize undesirable behavior.

Create a personal notebook:

Have your students decorate the outside of a paper report folder, the type with three clasps and a pocket inside each cover. Then, have each student write three to five positive comments about each person in the class. Encourage them to avoid such clichés as "You are nice" and "You are sweet." The students then insert all of the comments written about them into their individual books. It is a great way for class members to bond, as well as reduce challenges with peer pressure and minimize conflict. It is sure to become a lifelong, treasured item.

Have a "Star Student" of the week:

Choose one or two students every week to be "Star Students." Hang their pictures on a bulletin board with lists of things like their favorite activities, foods, colors, and songs. They can also be the "special helpers" during the time period they are chosen for.

Lindsay's Favorite Chicken Wings[8]

Lindsay Roberts

2 lbs. chicken wings

$^1\!/_2$ cup brown sugar

$^1\!/_2$ cup granulated sugar

$^1\!/_2$ cup soy sauce (Tamari is an excellent healthy alternative for those who might need a replacement for soy sauce)

1 cup chicken broth

Wash chicken, pat dry, and set aside.

In baking dish, mix all other ingredients and add chicken. Be sure all pieces are well coated. Cover.

Refrigerate to marinate for at least 2 hours, overnight if possible for best flavor.

Bake uncovered at 400° for 45 minutes. Serve warm or cold.

Humpty Dumpty Sat on a Wall

Lindsay Roberts

He heals the brokenhearted and binds up their wounds.
—Psalm 147:3

Do you remember the nursery rhyme "Humpty Dumpty"?

> Humpty Dumpty sat on a wall;
> Humpty Dumpty had a great fall;
> All the king's horses
> And all the king's men
> Couldn't put Humpty together again.

Here you have a splattered egg, and nobody could help him. What a mess!

If you turn the rhyme around, it may help you understand God and mankind. When God created man, He put him on a wall of His perfect protection in the Garden of Eden. Then sin got into man's eyes, and he couldn't see God. Sin got into his heart, and he couldn't believe God. He fell right off the wall of God's protection. What a mess!

When through Adam all of mankind fell into sin, all the king's horses and all the king's men—all the prophets throughout the Old Testament—did everything they knew to do, but they couldn't put mankind back together again. *It took a king.* In fact, it took more than just *a* king. It took *the* King. *It took the King of Kings and Lord of Lords—Jesus!*

Without God, our lives are a mess, and nothing in this world can fix us and make us right. But God sent Jesus to rescue us from the powers of darkness. And not only does He fix us, He makes us new. We are complete in Him.[9]

make **your** day count

Is your life broken? Does it seem beyond repair? Jesus is your King of Kings, the One who can make you whole. Go to Him, and let Him not only put you together again, but make you a new person in Christ.

Mama Said

Shanna D. Gregor

*By faith we understand that the worlds were framed
by the word of God, so that the things which are
seen were not made of things which are visible.*
—Hebrews 11:3 NKJV

My mother knew a secret. Perhaps she learned it from her
mother; nevertheless, she understood the power and impact
her words carried in my life. Just as God created the earth
and all that is in it with His faith-filled words, we have the
power to shape and mold the hearts of those whom God has
entrusted to us.

My mother gave me confidence through her words. She
always said, "Shanna, if you think you can, you can." When I
started school, I knew she expected excellent grades. Her
words still ring in my ears, "You can do anything you set your
heart and mind to. You can be anything you want to be when
you grow up."

As a result, I believed her words and found them to be
true. I put action to her faith in me. And I have done the
same with my own children. And just as I believed my
mother, they believe me.

As a teacher, you have a very similar power in the lives of
your students. Be quick to voice the faith you have in them,

and as they repeatedly hear your confident expectations, they
will begin to believe those words and go on to do great
things. Recognize the potential God has placed in each of
your students, and tell them what you see.

make **your** day count

Make a list of your students and beside each name, write down the potential
you see. For those particularly difficult students, ask God to show you what
He sees and what gifts He has placed within them. Then write short notes
to each student, stating your confidence in the gifts you see in them.

time **saving** tips

Ways to Simplify Your Life

Sometimes the simplest things can make life and your classroom run smoother.

Clean out and organize your desk:
Don't just stack those papers on the corner of your desk. Sift through them and throw away or file what you won't need immediately. Clutter triggers stress.

Make all of your copies one day ahead of time:
One trip to the copier is better than fifty. Tab all your books with the necessary pages and make the copies all at once. You can even plan ahead and make your copies for other lessons, keeping any leftovers in the book for later use.

Stick to one Day Timer®:
This doesn't mean to keep one Day Timer® for each class, car, or desk. One day timer is sufficient to handle your personal responsibilities as well as those for the school. The key is to get one sufficient in size and flexible enough with compartments to adapt to various aspects of your life's routines. Keep it simple.

Don't sweat the small stuff:
Don't worry about becoming "Super Teacher." With experience you will find what works for you.

Mixed Vegetable Casserole

2 small packages (32 oz. total) frozen, mixed vegetables
   (corn, carrots, green beans)
1 cup celery, chopped
1 cup onion, chopped
1 cup cheddar cheese, shredded
1 cup mayonnaise
8–10 Ritz crackers, crumbled (can use saltines or herbed
   stuffing mix)
$\frac{1}{2}$ –1 whole stick butter, melted

Mix all together and put into greased 1 $\frac{1}{2}$ -quart casserole dish.

Sprinkle cracker crumbs over top.

Pour butter over all.

Bake 30 minutes at 350°.

Serves 8–10.

time **saving** tips

More Ways to Simplify Your Life

Schedule a day to leave on time and stick to it:

Though the bell may ring at 3:00 P.M., we all know that teacher's *do not* get off work then. Select a day that you would like to leave earlier than usual and then stick to it. Not everything *has* to be done in the classroom, and a change of scenery might be just what you need.

Open mail close to a wastebasket:

Toss junk mail into file thirteen the minute you open it. For bills, discard the outer envelopes along with any unwanted inserts. Establish a designated place for coupons and special offers.

Avoid subscribing to things you don't have time to read:

Mailboxes fill up with a vast variety of catalogs and magazines, leading to a cluttered desk and guilt over good intentions. Only subscribe to what you know you can read, and free your mind for more productive and rewarding matters!

Avoid getting involved in unnecessary school politics:

Politics are everywhere; when feasible steer clear of getting involved. You will save yourself stress and pointless worry.

easy **recipes**

Pumpkin Butter and Muffins

Abby Detcher

Pumpkin Butter

1 cup canned pumpkin
½ cup sugar
1½ tsp. pumpkin pie spice

Combine all in a saucepan and simmer over medium heat
   until sugar is dissolved.

Pour into a container and chill.

Pumpkin Muffins

2 cups flour
⅓ cup white sugar
½ tsp. salt
¼ tsp. baking soda
½ cup canned pumpkin
⅓ cup buttermilk*

⅔ cup packed brown sugar
1 Tbsp. baking powder
1 tsp. cinnamon
½ cup butter, melted
2 large eggs

Melt butter in microwave. Add in pumpkin and eggs, then
   buttermilk.

Beat until smooth.

Add dry ingredients. Mix by hand until just mixed.

Bake at 400° for 20 minutes. Makes 12 yummy, plump muffins.

*If you do not have buttermilk, measure milk to just about ⅓ cup
and add 1 tsp. lemon juice and let stand for 5 minutes.

The Power to Bless

Karen Hardin

Death and life are in the power of the tongue.
—Proverbs 18:21 NKJV

It wasn't a routine assignment. To me, it was actually pretty fun compared to the general run-of-the-mill seatwork. I finished quickly and turned in my paper. "That was fun," I said, handing it to the teacher.

As I turned to return to my desk, the teacher called out in a voice dripping with sarcasm, "Class, Karen has just informed me how *much* she enjoyed this assignment and that we should do more like it."

The heat of embarrassment flooded over me. In the seventh grade, the last thing I wanted was to be singled out, but to be publicly ridiculed by a teacher was mortifying. Several class-mates snickered and made rude comments, the teacher making no attempt to stop the cruelty she had initiated.

Unfortunately, that moment affected my interaction with other teachers for the next several years. In one instant, trust and my eagerness to learn had received a critical blow.

Today, as an adult and through my walk with Christ, I look back and can offer forgiveness and grace. Through Christ healing has come. But I have often wondered what was going on in that teacher's life to trigger such an unwarranted, stinging remark.

As teachers what we say has a tremendous impact on our students. We have the ability to encourage and build them up or to reject and demoralize them. It is an awesome responsibility. Let's choose to bless.

make **your** day count

Make a list of your students. Write down an encouraging
word to share with each one. Make a point to share this
special word with at least one student a day per class.
Make a new list each month and watch your students blossom.

Let Your Life Do the Preaching

Darla Satterfield Davis

You are our epistle written in our hearts, known and read by all men; clearly you are an epistle of Christ.
—2 Corinthians 3:2,3 NKJV

In our low-income, public school, the superintendent suggested that we could honor the separation of church and state as well as help our students more by *living* our convictions rather than preaching them. One day after detention, the roughest boy in my class met me at my car. "Mrs. Davis…I was, uh, wantin' to ask you about…God…but I don't want to get you in trouble or nothin'."

Stepping outside the schoolyard—but still in a widely visible area—I said, "Sure, Billy. It's okay for us to talk about this since we're not on the school grounds and it's after hours. I'm going to talk with you as a friend, not as your teacher."

Having witnessed something in my life that he wanted, Billy proceeded to ask all kinds of questions. Finally, I asked if I could pray for him. He agreed, and together we invited Jesus into his heart. Pretending not to see his tears, I added, "Billy, I'm looking for great things from you. You are special to God and to me."

I wouldn't be surprised to hear news of Billy doing great and noteworthy things. Worth far more to me, however, is the fact that he has already beat the odds of his circumstances. He graduated from high school, is happily married, and today I have the privilege of teaching his child. The most important thing about Billy's life, however, is that he has a personal relationship with Jesus Christ. What greater achievement is there than a life won for the kingdom of God?

make **your** day count

Today, let your actions speak louder than your words in reflecting God's love, patience, and integrity to your students as well as the faculty. Let your light shine so brightly that people can't help but recognize that there's something wonderfully different about you!

Unexpected Blessings

Holly Sonnenschein

"Give, and it will be given to you. A good measure,
pressed down, shaken together and
running over, will be poured into your lap."
—Luke 6:38

Teachers are givers. We are constantly giving instruction, discipline, encouragement, guidance, love, support, an open ear, our energy, our time. The list is endless, even when our resources are not. And each of us needs to feel that what we do matters, that we are making a difference in the lives of our students. As teachers we know how good it feels to know that our efforts are appreciated and that we are loved.

The cute little Christmas and birthday presents are always special, but those unexpected gifts—such as a hug, a flower from the garden, a beautifully written card, a piece of fruit, or a spontaneous gesture of thanks from an appreciative parent—touch my heart the most. Unexpected blessings like these let me know during the hard times that yes, what I do counts. Someone notices. Someone cares.

Our students can also benefit from spontaneous, unexpected acts of kindness. They may not recognize or appreciate many of our efforts until they reach adulthood, but there are some things we can do now that will make an immediate impact and help them feel the deep love we have for them.

We can demonstrate to them how much we cherish them just as their extra-mile efforts touch our hearts.

Acknowledging a student's award, celebrating a team win, or just verbalizing your appreciation makes students feel special. Showing up at a sporting event and cheering on the students is sure to warm the heart. Why not bring in donuts one morning or pass out freshly popped popcorn or mini chocolate candy bars? How about a few extra minutes at recess?

We all need to feel loved and cherished. Do something extra and unexpected for your students today.

make **your** day count

Find a way to bless your students today in a way that will surprise them and make them smile. And don't forget to verbalize how much you care.

time **saving** tips

Stress Relief

Try these strategies for a more peaceful life.

Get plenty of sleep:
No one functions best when sleep deprived. Getting enough rest will not only help relieve stress, but it will also help you avoid that nasty cold that is going around.

Be on time:
Consider setting your clock at home a couple of minutes ahead of the actual time to give yourself a psychological cushion.

Slow down:
Purposely slow your breathing and take full breaths. Walk, talk, and drive at a slower pace. Life isn't a race.

Come in early to prepare for the day:
Having to stop in the middle of class to find a book or make copies can be a hassle and breaks synergy with both the teacher and the students.

Kick your shoes off:
Take a minute or two to kick off your shoes, lean your head back, and close your eyes for a full minute. It will work miracles for you!

Invest in a comfortable chair:
It's well worth the money to invest in a good, comfortable chair. Make sure to acquire one that will allow you to lean your head back for a moment of silence. It should also provide sufficient back support.

easy **recipes**

Ants in a Boat
Cleo Justus

This is a nice low sugar after school snack or an easy class project.

Wash and cut celery sticks into 6-inch pieces.

Lay on paper towel to dry.

Spread hollow inside of celery stick with cream cheese (or low fat cream cheese) and top with raisins.

Don't Get Stressed Out, Stand Still!

Lindsay Roberts

Fear ye not, stand still, and see the salvation of the LORD.
—Exodus 14:13 KJV

Are you so overwhelmed by everything you need to accomplish that you feel as though you might crack? I understand what it's like to be stressed out. It's difficult to find balance in our lives with our hectic schedules and multitude of responsibilities.

Fear is a major cause of stress, yet there are many places in the Bible where God tells us to "fear ye not." When we "fear not," we are able to step outside the realm of being panic-stricken by circumstances. It is then that we can "stand still" as He instructs.

Have you ever tried to make sense to a person who is running around all stressed out? In contrast, if you will stand still and get into an atmosphere of faith and trust in God, you will "see the salvation of the Lord."

When I looked up this Scripture in the original text, I found that it means, "One who comes from outside to bring help." When you're in the middle of a stressful situation, the problems are often all you can see. Of course, if you were in the middle of a fire, the situation would look really bad to you. But if you were *outside* the fire, you would be able to handle it more rationally. God deals with your circumstances from outside the stress, so step outside with Him. He has the solution you need![10]

make **your** day count

Make a conscious effort to "step outside" your circumstances today and stand with God. As you rest and "stand still" with Him, He will intervene in your circumstances and work things out for your good.

Organizational Aids

Darla Satterfield Davis

The Teacher's Survival Kit

Keep this kit close at hand. Some items to put in it might include aspirin, antacids, cough drops, breath mints, wet wipes, Band Aids, antibacterial lotion, a needle and thread, safety pins, a tube of superglue, a small tooth-brush and toothpaste, a comb and mirror, feminine products, clear nail polish for runs in pantyhose, an extra pair of pantyhose, correct change for the phone or pop machines, an extra car door key, and even a small tool set.

Survival Kit for Substitute Teachers

This kit is always pinned on the wall by my desk, flagged in big bold letters. In the event that I must be absent unexpectedly, it contains all the vital information any sub would need:

A personal note welcoming the sub along with an inspirational book-mark as a token gift.

A list of class helpers.

Any health issues of students.

Seating charts.

Emergency information sheet: fire drill routes, nurse contact informa-tion, location of first-aid kit.

List of class rules.

Master copies of various assignments and review pages.

Incentives for good behavior such as special books or videos to be used at the end of the day.

Baked Spaghetti

Lisa Anne Camille Louissaint

1 lb. ground beef
$\frac{1}{2}$ onion chopped
1 lb. spaghetti noodles
1 28-oz. can of prepared pasta sauce
8 oz. sharp cheddar cheese
$\frac{1}{2}$ cup grated parmesan cheese (not the canned kind)

Season and brown beef.

Add onions and cook another 5 minutes.

Boil spaghetti until al dente and drain.

Combine spaghetti with beef mixture and sauce. Mix well.

Pour into 9 x 13 inch greased casserole dish, top with cheeses, and bake for about 15–20 minutes until brown and bubbly.

Serve with a salad and garlic bread.

time **saving** tips

More Organizational Aids

Darla Satterfield Davis

"You lost my paper!"

Avoid possible accusations by picking up all the papers and stapling them together. Grade and record them while they are still stapled, and do not pull apart until you are ready to return them. In addition, if you assign a number to each of your students, you will know immediately if a page is missing.

Keep a schedule notebook:

If you find yourself in a situation where you teach many different classes on differing days, it might be wise to keep a schedule notebook. Take a three-ring binder and use dividers to separate into different days. In plastic sheet protectors, put a schedule of your classes under each section. Also include a list of class rules, fire drill information, and intercom numbers. Include a diagram of your room with a sheeting chart for each class.

Keep your students organized:

Start by making each student a colored folder for each of the classes you teach. In each folder, they can keep blank paper and returned work. When it is time to study for a test, all of their work is already in the folder for them to review. After each chapter, clean out the folders and start over again.

Make Your Own Bubbles!

Amanda Pilgrim

A fun classroom project.

Sunshine Bubbles

2 cups Joy® dishwashing liquid

6 cups water

$\frac{1}{2}$ cup corn syrup

Mix together and let set over night

Long Lasting Bubbles

1 oz Dawn® dishwashing liquid

1 oz Glycerin

1 cup water

Mix together. Mixture will have a very thick consistency.

No Tears Bubbles

$\frac{1}{2}$ cup baby shampoo

$\frac{1}{2}$ cup water

3 tablespoons of corn syrup

Mix together and let set a few hours

My Mountain Was Actually a Molehill

Karen Hardin

Each of you should look not only to your own interests,
but also to the interests of others.

—Philippians 2:4

Lily entered to drop off her late assignment. With a mountain of papers to grade, I was slightly annoyed by the interruption, but turned to accept her work. Untypical of this sanguine student, she was quiet and reluctant to leave. She obviously had something on her mind, but the mountain before me beckoned.

If I stop to talk, I'll never get these papers graded on time, I reasoned, waving good-bye even as my conscience tugged at my heart.

I attempted to resume my grading, but to no avail. All I could concentrate on was Lily's somber face. I grabbed my coat and ran toward her dorm, finding her halfway there.

"Hey, what's up?" I asked, reaching out to take her hand. Tears filled her eyes as the weight she had been carrying spilled out. "The doctor... an eye condition...." Away from home for the first time, Lily just needed someone to listen to and comfort her. She wanted her mom, but I would do.

"Can I pray with you?" I asked immediately.

Lily nodded. "I was hoping you would. I think I need to finally trust God."

As we prayed together, Lily accepted Christ into her heart. We hugged as she wiped away her tears and left.

And to think—I almost missed a moment for eternity because a mountain of papers temporarily blocked my view.

make **your** day count

It's easy to get overwhelmed with the daily tasks of teaching and overlook the greater responsibility towards the hearts of our students. Observe your students today, asking God to help you recognize which ones could use an uplifting word. Ask one or two how they are doing, and be ready to listen.

Keep Them on the Edge of Their Seats

Holly Sonnenschein

*Only be careful, and watch yourselves closely so that you
do not forget the things your eyes have seen or let them
slip from your heart as long as you live. Teach them to
your children and to their children after them.*

—Deuteronomy 4:9

As teachers, we are given the opportunity to open up our students' minds to learning and their hearts to God's amazing plan. Whether we teach in a public or a private school setting, we are teaching about His wondrous design. We have reason to be excited about what we teach! I always try to make classes fun and enjoyable by using object lessons and staying excited about the subject matter. I purposely speak with an enthusiastic tone of voice and stay animated to keep the students on the edge of their seats. My goal is to teach in such a way that it makes them hang on to every word I say.

Once when I was teaching science, I took my students outside to collect leaf samples. We marveled at the many varieties of trees, comparing how some were similar and others not. We studied the leaves of each type of tree and how intricately they were formed. We noted that no single leaf was exactly like any other.

The next day, one of the students came in with a huge grocery bag full of various kinds of leaves he had collected on his own! The huge smile on his face and eagerness to share what he had found were priceless. Similarly, when I taught on insects one time, a student came in the next day with a huge Goliath beetle! The whole class was amazed.

We can draw our students in! We have the ability to bring life and excitement to everything we teach, so don't hold back.

make **your** day count

Enthusiasm is contagious, and that is something
we definitely want our students to catch! If teaching is
not as enjoyable as it once was, ask God to help you see the
subject matter as He sees it. After all, He is the author of it all!

If My People Will Pray

Lindsay Roberts

If my people, who are called by my name, will humble
themselves and pray and seek my face and turn from
their wicked ways, then will I hear from heaven
and will forgive their sin and will heal their land.
—2 Chronicles 7:14

God wants to do amazing and wonderful things in our personal lives, in our nation, and in our world. And we have a part to play in order for Him to do this. One way we can help to usher in revival and bring peace in the midst of chaos is to humble ourselves and pray. Notice that this verse says, "If *my* people...." God's people are those who are committed to Him and follow His ways.

That sentence goes on to say, "and turn from their wicked ways." If things are amiss in our lives and if we want God to heal us, we need to humble ourselves before Him, ask Him to forgive us, and turn from any ungodly ways. Instead of spending time watching programs or videos that contradict biblical values, consider spending time on your knees before the face of an awesome and powerful God. He is available to meet you at any hour of the day or night.

These are dangerous times, and we must be in a place of prayer and have a prayer covering. We *have* to have a Power

Source greater than this world, and that Source is Jesus Christ—the Prince of Peace, King of kings, and Lord of lords.

I believe God is calling us together as a body of believers to get the garbage out of our lives. Because when we do, the Holy Spirit of God can rise up inside of us, and we can be a beacon of light to a dark and troubled world. We sing about being a light in darkness. Now let's do it![11]

make **your** day count

Even if you only have five or ten minutes, take some time today to humble yourself before God. Ask Him to reveal any of your ways that don't please Him, and then turn from them. Pray for Him to draw our nation to Himself and heal our land.

time **saving** tips

Classroom Management

If you manage your classroom well, you'll spend much less time investing in damage control and navigating through challenging situations. Think and act proactively!

Assign jobs to students:

Tasks may not get completed as well as if you did them yourself, but you will have less to think about. Giving students responsibility can be incredibly valuable, as it strengthens self-esteem. Your students will also begin to take pride in their classroom and feel as though they have become an integral part of the system.

Create a platform to air out problems privately:

Challenges will arise between students. Having a known and pre-arranged platform for students to air out their concerns will eliminate unnecessary discord in the classroom. Try having students inform you when a problem is perceived and set up a meeting time in a neutral environment where you can act as a mediator.

Make available a suggestion/problem box:

Some students may feel intimidated about telling you there is a dilemma or offering a creative idea. Having a place available where they have the opportunity to anonymously inform you of a situation or ingenious idea can make them more comfortable.

easy **recipes**

Cheese Ball

Laverna Satterfield

2 8-oz. packages of cream cheese
$\frac{1}{2}$ cup grated cheddar cheese
$\frac{1}{2}$ of a bell pepper, finely chopped
3 to 4 Tbsp. of finely chopped onion
2 Tbsp. of Worcestershire sauce
1 jar dried beef, minced
Chopped pecans

Mix all together and form into a ball.

Refrigerate until firm.

Roll in chopped pecans.

Half of this recipe also makes a nice-sized cheese ball.

In Everything Give Thanks

Holly Sonnenschein

Be joyful always; pray continually; give thanks in all circumstances, for this is God's will for you in Christ Jesus.
—1 Thessalonians 5:16–18

Our professions can become overwhelming at times. There are moments when I feel like I will never catch up. Whether it is turning grades in, grading papers, calling parents, making lesson plans, creating projects, or cleaning the classroom, teachers have a lot to do—not to mention life *outside* of school!

If I'm not careful, I find myself complaining—first internally, then verbally. Then it can become a habit, and before I know it, everything begins to look dull and gray. The joy of teaching gets buried somewhere under a pile of term papers on my desk.

During one particularly challenging day, I took my class outside for recess, and there before us was a young boy swinging without a care in the world. He was simply looking up at the sky and belting out the song, "He's Got the Whole World in His Hands." The scene captured my attention and changed my day.

The boy was a familiar face at our school and was known for his very distinct limp and a few other handicaps. Yet to him, none of that mattered. He was so full of joy on that swing that all he could do was sing. Suddenly it hit me that the secret of this boy's joy was that in spite of his circumstances, he was thankful and full of praise!

There in the midst of my seemingly gray day was a bright ray of sunshine in the form of a thankful little boy. It helped me to put things into perspective, and whenever I feel the gray clouds rolling in, I reflect back to that moment and whisper a word of thanks to an awesome God.

make **your** day count

List some of the things you are thankful for. Then imagine your life *without* those things. Most likely you will find that you have much more to be thankful for than you have to complain about. Stay in an attitude of thanks all day! You'll be glad you did.

A Tough Little Philly in Texas

Darla Satterfield Davis

A gentle answer turns away wrath,
but a harsh word stirs up anger.
—Proverbs 15:1

The first time I saw Terrie's mother, she came out literally kicking and screaming as a couple of policemen escorted her out of the elementary school. She was a fireball from "Philly," and our little Texas town had never seen the likes of her.

Parent/teacher conference night soon followed, and I dreaded the encounter. I earnestly sought the Lord about it because I was genuinely concerned about Terrie, yet I didn't want a repeat performance from her mother. The following day I sensed God leading me to handle the conference assertively.

"Hi! I'm Mrs. Davis. I've been so anxious to meet you," I said cheerfully as I came from behind my desk to greet her. "Let me close this door so we can really talk." Before she could start in with her usual discourse, I said, "It is so encouraging when parents care about their kids and keep tabs on them like you do. Now," I continued, hardly drawing a breath, "I need your advice. After all, no one knows Terri better than you, right?"

She nodded and sat staring at me.

"I need your input on the best way to handle her when she disrupts class or doesn't complete her assignments." I sat ready to take notes.

Taken aback she stammered a bit before she began listing consequences she felt I could use. She ended by patting me on the knee and assuring me that if Terrie didn't do exactly as I told her, I was to let her know, and she would take care of it.

Things began to turn around for Terri, and from that day until this, whenever I see her mother, she greets me and begins talking like we are old friends. The wisdom of God works wonders.

make **your** day count

Think of some ways to improve your parent/teacher conferences and jot them down for later reference. Ask God to give you wisdom in your dealings with difficult people including your students, their parents, and members of the faculty.

time **saving** tips

Successful Parent/Teacher Conferences

There is no need to fear a parent/teacher conference. Use this time to get the parents on the same page with you. Making an ally out of the parents can improve life in the classroom.

Exhibit a positive and upbeat disposition:

This will go a long way in disarming angry parents. Often loud and aggressive people just need to feel they are being heard. Make it clear that you are on the same team working *with* them for the benefit of their child.

Begin with something positive:

Conferences are difficult for parents as well. Begin by acknowledging the strengths of their child, and then slowly move into areas that need improvement.

Stick to the facts:

Tell the parents about the situation concerning their child, and allow them to make the obvious conclusions.

Have all documentation and paperwork available:

Always bring your grade book, samples of the child's work, and any significant paperwork to the meeting with you. Write down items that require follow-up.

Don't surprise parents with grades:

Parents should be aware of their child's progress long before the end of the term. Contact parents when grades first begin to slip. If a parent doesn't know there is a problem, he or she can't help solve it.

Lindsay's Guacamole Dip[12]

Lindsay Roberts

5 avocados, peeled and with pits removed
$\frac{1}{2}$ large tomato, chopped
$\frac{1}{2}$ onion (Vidalia, if possible), diced
Sea salt to taste
Juice of $\frac{1}{2}$ lemon, freshly squeezed
Roughly chopped cilantro, to taste (optional)

Place in food processor and pulse a few seconds until the
mixture is blended together.

Serve chilled.

Store with one pit placed in the center to help keep it from
turning brown.

time **saving** tips

More Tips for Successful Parent/Teacher Conferences

 Stay on the subject:

Although it is important to establish a rapport with parents, stay in control of the discussion.

 Offer potential solutions:

By presenting ideas that could benefit their child, you increase the chances of having parental support at home. Have available a list of tutors, or offer to send home extra study sheets and/or projects for grade recovery or improvement.

 Don't overwhelm parents with information:

Parents often come straight from work to a conference and are frequently exhausted from the day. Simplify as much as possible. Written examples are tremendously effective and are great to send home after the discussion.

 Stick to time schedules:

Begin on time, be prepared, and finish on time. If information has not been covered due to time restraints, then schedule a second appointment with the intent to "follow up on progress." Not only will parents appreciate your respect for their time, but you will more likely secure follow-through on future meetings scheduled if it is perceived that you anticipate positive resolve.

 Create a non-threatening environment:

Instead of sitting behind your desk, sit next to the parents at a table. This will foster a sense of comradery and help put the parents at ease.

Tortilla Rollups

Laverna Satterfield and Wilma Wright

8 oz. sour cream
8 oz. cream cheese
Small can chopped green chilies
Small can chopped black olives
Grated cheddar cheese (or cheddar and jack cheese)
Finely chopped green onion
Flour Tortillas
Picante Sauce

Mix and spread on flour tortillas and roll.

Let set in refrigerator for several hours or overnight.

Slice and serve with picante sauce.

Olives, cheese, and onion quantities can vary based on preference.

A Calling

Georgia Lee Paul

Having then gifts differing according to the grace that is given to us, let us use them: if prophecy, let us prophesy in proportion to our faith; or ministry, let us use it in our ministering; he who teaches, in teaching.

—Romans 12:6,7 NKJV

I attended Oral Roberts University to get my education degree because I knew that not only would I receive an excellent education, I would also learn about teaching from a biblical perspective. In our first education class, we did not even open the textbook for the whole first week! We studied the Bible to learn what God intended our profession to be—a calling. More than any other factor, that one week has had the greatest impact on my view of what it means to be a teacher.

I saw the value that God places on teachers and the influence we could have on our students for eternity. I learned that I could pray for my students every day before they arrived and that God would give me wisdom and insight into any struggles they were facing. I was encouraged to pray for my classroom, that it would circumvent many behavioral problems. Before my time at ORU, it never occurred to me that I could do any of these things. It was also very enlightening to discover that I could actually be anointed by the Holy

Spirit to teach, just as a minister is anointed to preach. Both are callings from God, and He equips the teacher to teach just as much as He equips a pastor to preach.

These are just a few of the many reasons that I consider it an awesome privilege to have attended a Christian university like ORU. That first week was over eight years ago, yet every day I put into practice the principles I learned there. It is to this and to relying on the Holy Spirit that I attribute any success I have attained.

make **your** day count

Arrive early to class and pray over your classroom, from the doorway to the students' desks to your own. Ask God to fill your classroom with His peace.

Ask for wisdom and insight into each student's academic success.

Ask for guidance, wisdom, and anointing as you fulfill your calling to teach.

What Are You Filling Up On?

Lindsay Roberts

Above all else, guard your heart,
for it is the wellspring of life.
—Proverbs 4:23

It is vitally important what we put into our spirits. We are surrounded by television shows and movies that are filled with lust, curse words, and pornography. No matter how nicely they try to put it, little to no clothing on people slides into the category of pornography. When we take all of that into our spirits, we open ourselves up to all the turmoil of the world and over time become desensitized to ungodliness. Then we not only don't stop it, but we *embrace* it by watching it and even paying to be entertained by it.

Did you know that the word *video* comes from the Latin word meaning "to envy" or "be jealous"? What are you watching on television, at the movies, on the Internet? I am speaking to us as adults and believers, but you no doubt experience many behavioral problems in the classroom that can be traced back to this very issue. Is it any wonder that students are disruptive and have difficulty learning if they are being exposed to hours and hours of dark or ungodly entertainment?

Many Christians are well educated, well dressed, and well behaved. They declare Christianity with their mouths, but live lifestyles that speak otherwise. But it doesn't have to be this way. First we have to repent of the garbage we've allowed into our lives, then we must vigilantly guard our hearts, so the wellspring of life can flow through us.

What about your students? You don't have much control over what they are exposed to when they leave your class-room, but during the time you have them, let your light shine brightly. Hold forth a higher standard and let your life be a walking advertisement of the blessing of walking in God's ways.[13]

make **your** day count

Be especially mindful today of the things you allow yourself as well as your students to see and hear. Fill your eyes and ears—and those of your students—with good things that promote light, joy, peace, and love.

Spice Things Up

Holly Sonnenschein

Taste and see that the LORD is good.
—Psalm 34:8

God wants us to taste of His goodness every day, and it delights His heart to add special "seasonings" to spice things up for us. It blesses Him to see us delight in the children He's entrusted to our care. Perhaps it is a student finally grasping that concept you have been teaching or a young child wrapping his or her tiny arms around your waist. There is not a day that goes by that the Lord is not good! But it's up to us to taste of that goodness and see, or recognize, it at work in our lives!

One thing I do to spice things up for my class is to dedicate one day a month to a theme relating to that month. On these days, everything we do is geared around that subject. In September, for instance, we have an apple day. In May we have a flower day. In October we have a pumpkin day, which is probably my favorite.

Examples of the things we do on pumpkin day are to have the children count pumpkin seeds, which they then plant in a cup of soil. We use different measuring units to bake pumpkin bread. I might read a story about pumpkins, while the children draw pictures of them. We have even taken field trips to a pumpkin patch located near our school.

The most rewarding thing about these special days is watching the children's love for learning catch fire. It delights me to see them get excited about little things like changing a school day around just a little bit. Nothing brings me more joy than watching a child's face light up from new discoveries. It is through little things like these that I constantly taste of God's awesome goodness…and on pumpkin day, I even get to taste a little of that pumpkin bread too!

make **your** day count

Pick a theme for today and incorporate it into every subject you teach.
Then savor the delight you see in your students' faces.

time **saving** tips

Ways to Renew the Classroom Environment

Just as the air in a room can become stale and heavy, the feel of the classroom can sometimes become stagnant. Breathe new life into your classroom with these simple yet effective ideas.

Decorate for the different seasons:

Celebrate the differing seasons with your class by decorating your room. Class project items make great decorations, and there is no worry about storage space. Remember not to overdo it or spend a lot of your valuable time on decorating. Students love to help, and it instills in them a sense of pride in their classroom.

Place plants in various spots around your classroom:

Whether you bring them from home or grow some for a class project, plants add life, color, freshness, and much-needed oxygen to the atmosphere.

Make space for an aquarium:

The gentle sounds of an aquarium can help calm disruptive students and add a sense of tranquility to your classroom. It doesn't have to be elaborate; a simple goldfish in a bowl will do. What more delightful way to observe and enjoy the beauty of God's aquatic creatures and at the same time brighten up that empty corner in your room.

easy **recipes**

Classroom Pumpkin Pudding

Abby Detcher

This recipe works great in the classroom and can be a festive treat to celebrate fall.

Scoop out 1 Tbsp. pumpkin pie filling.
Add 3 shakes of cinnamon.
Count 5 raisins (if you like them).
Add 2 Tbsp. of milk.
Add 1 Tbsp. of instant vanilla pudding.
Stir and count to 25.
Add 1 Tbsp. of whipped cream.

Laugh Attack

Kim Lutherbeck

The cheerful heart has a continual feast.
—Proverbs 15:15

Laughter is such a wonderful tool to help us break through things that try to hold us down. Proverbs 15:13 NKJV says, "A merry heart makes a cheerful countenance." Proverbs 17:22 says it does us good like medicine. And Nehemiah 8:10 says that "the joy of the LORD is your strength." I know from personal experience that these things are true.

I'm sure you would agree, each day of class holds fresh challenges, and teachers are just like everyone else—we sometime bring the cares of the world into our workplace. If you're like me, there are times when you feel so overwhelmed that you can't think straight and it seems like everyone is dancing on your last nerve.

I was experiencing one of those days when the Lord taught me a valuable lesson. I sensed Him say to me, *You need to have a laugh attack!*

"What's a laugh attack?" I asked.

What He taught me that day was priceless, and I've used it every school year since.

When things just aren't going right in class, or if the children seem to be out of control, or if we just need a break from stress, we have a laugh attack! We actually sit in a circle, and at the count of three, we laugh! In the beginning, of course, the laughs are forced, but before long the joy of the Lord begins to flow. If nothing else, we laugh at our own silliness. It is amazing what freedom comes during one of these times. Laughter indeed gives your heart a continual feast!

make **your** day count

Make you day count! Release the joy of the Lord in your classroom today—or even in your car, if you need it personally—and institute a laugh attack. It may seem awkward at first, but if you'll stick with it, you'll begin to sense pressure lift and things turn around.

Giving Your Life

Emily Biffle

[Jesus said,] "Greater love has no one than this,
that he lay down his life for his friends."
—John 15:13

We have a tremendous opportunity to model and teach our students life principles that are pleasing to the Lord. One of the most important is in the area of giving. First, we set an example by giving of ourselves to our students every day. We can also teach them and lead them in giving of themselves to their neighbors.

It will require planning and many times coordinating with administrators of various organizations, but try doing some of these as a way for your class to give of yourselves:

- Visit a nursing home.
- Adopt an elderly person living in a nursing home or a shut-in.
- Collect blankets and distribute them to the homeless.
- Buy groceries for a family in need.
- Visit children in the hospital.
- Collect change for a charity of choice.
- Make cards for people in the hospital.

- Visit a shelter.

- Sing carols, or do a concert for the less advantaged.

- Help feed meals to the homeless.

- Rake leaves for widows and single mothers.

- Bag groceries at a food bank.

- Ask your class for ideas.

It is common for kids to complain about not getting that pair of hundred-dollar tennis shoes or not getting to buy every video game that hits the market. Teaching your students to think beyond themselves and making them aware of the needs of others will open their hearts and help them recognize how very much they have to be thankful for.

Giving of their lives to others will make a lasting impression on your students, and the rewards they take from their experiences will be priceless. They will be changed, and so will you!

make **your** day count

Talk to your students about giving today, and begin making plans for a field trip to give of yourselves as a class.

time **saving** tips

More Ways to Renew the Classroom Environment

Take your class for a walk around the building:

What a surprising treat for your class! Take a few moments to take a short jaunt and enjoy the change of scenery. The fresh air and short break from studies will reenergize your students and help them to shake off any unproductive heaviness.

Teach a lesson outside:

Have your class sit on the grass as you read them a story, or have an art lesson on sketching a tree. Whether you are teaching a lesson on nature or just needing a change of pace, both you and your students will feel revitalized and ready to tackle the next activity.

Play music:

It is said that classical music stimulates brain function. Keep a CD player and an assortment of soothing music to play while your students do seatwork. Try upbeat music to energize the class for spring cleaning.

Amazing Cookie Bars

Laverna Satterfield

½ cup margarine
1 ½ cups vanilla wafer crumbs
1 cup chopped walnuts
1 cup (6 oz.) chocolate chips
1 ⅓ cups flaked coconut
1 can Eagle Brand Sweetened Condensed Milk

Pour melted butter into bottom of 9 x 13 inch pan.

Sprinkle wafer crumbs over melted butter.

Sprinkle chopped nuts over crumbs and press down gently.

Scatter chocolate chips over nuts and press down firmly.

Sprinkle coconut over all.

Pour Eagle Brand milk evenly over coconut.

Bake at 350° for 25 minutes or until lightly browned on top.

Cool in pan for 15 minutes and cut into bars.

time **saving** tips

More Ways to Renew the Classroom Environment

Don't get stuck in a rut:

Don't limit yourself by becoming trapped in a daily routine. Spice up the day by changing things around. Whether it's altering the usual order of events or simply modifying seating for an activity. Plan surprises for your students. If you are excited, they will be too.

Rearrange the furniture:

Try new things with the furniture in your classroom. Have students sit in groups or form a semi-circle around the board. Don't think that the way you set your classroom up at the beginning of the year is the same way it has to stay till the end of it. Try creating centers to change the look of your room. A section of the room with a couple of pillows or beanbag chairs on the floor makes a great free reading area.

No-Bake Peanut Butter Cookies[14]

1 cup honey
1 cup sugar or natural sugar substitute
2 cups peanut butter
4–5 cups corn flakes

Melt honey and sugar together and stir until boiling.

Remove from heat.

Stir in peanut butter, then add corn flakes.*

Drop by spoonfuls onto waxed paper. Let cool.

*Other cereals such as quick-cooking oats, rice, or corn can also be used.

God Knows What Will Work

Darla Satterfield Davis

The LORD *gives wisdom, and from his mouth*
come knowledge and understanding.
—Proverbs 2:6

Julia was exasperated. "It seems that I can hardly believe a word Karen says! And no punishment I dole out seems to make any difference."

"All of your foster kids have required time and patience as they've settled in," I reminded. "We'll win Karen over too." I thought a moment, and an idea came to me, which I offered carefully, "Maybe punishment isn't the answer."

As Karen's teacher, I had let her imagination run wild in her creative writing assignments, but knew we had to insist on the plain truth otherwise. I decided to run the idea by Julia.

"What would you think about letting Karen come to the Bible study I hold on Friday nights? It's just for kids, and we've been talking about Lucifer and why he was cast out of heaven. Maybe Karen would like to come."

Sure enough, Karen wanted to come, and that Friday night she sat spellbound as I recounted the biblical story. I emphasized how Satan had lied to the angels and then to Eve and what a terrible price had been required because of it.

"Satan is the father of lies," I stressed, then added, "and we don't want to be like him, do we?"

It was only a small beginning, but Karen's eyes softened and filled with tears that night. I knew God was at work and that things were going to work out fine.

God knows our hearts and what correction will be most effective for us. If we seek His will in dealing with others, He will give us His wisdom.

make **your** day count

Are you dealing with a student who is not responding to your current methods? Ask God to give you wisdom and insight into this student's life. Each child is a creation of God, and He knows how to get through to them. Ask Him to show you the most effective plan.

A Glorious Crown

Georgia Lee Paul

*Shepherd God's flock, for whom you are responsible. Watch
over them because you want to, not because you are forced....
Do it because you are happy to serve, not because you want
money. Do not be like a ruler over people you are responsible
for, but be good examples to them. Then when Christ, the
Chief Shepherd, comes, you will get a glorious crown.*

—1 Peter 5:2–4 NCV

One day when I was at Oral Roberts University studying
to be an elementary teacher, this passage jumped off the page
at me. I knew that it would be my foundation as an educator.
I saw that God would give me students to watch over and
that I was to find joy in it. I was to serve my class gladly and
not focus on my salary. I was to set an example, not be a
harsh dictator. Then, as a result of the lives that would be
changed, His reward would never fade.

Soon after this revelation, I went with ORU on a mission
trip to South Africa, where our team was able to go into
many schools. I had a couple of opportunities to speak to the
teachers, and I told them that I was studying to be a teacher. I
honored them for the job they were doing and then shared
these verses with them.

The missionary we were working with happened to be
writing curriculum for these teachers, and when she learned

of the passage that I was sharing with them, she told me that she wanted to put it on the front page of all her curriculum!

Now, as a classroom teacher, I use these verses in the letter that I send to the parents at the start of each school year. They are verses I live by.

make **your** day count

Meditate on the verses that were shared and evaluate where you stand in following them. Commit to change any wrong attitudes or actions, then ask God to help you do it.

time **saving** tips

Classroom Treats

Linda Burritt

Trail mix is always a hit. In a large bowl, mix together a large bag of M&Ms, a large box of raisins, and a large can of cocktail peanuts. (Make sure none of your students are allergic to peanuts before giving this treat to your class. Cashews or even salted sunflower seeds are possible substitutions.)

Give each student a napkin and a handful. The combination of sweet and salty is a treat for the taste buds! If there is any left over, which is unlikely, it can be stored in an airtight container, such as a metal coffee can with a lid.

Try rewarding your students with this simple treat: Pass a bag of pretzels around the class, letting each student take two or three. Then take a couple of containers of ready-made cake icing around to each one, so they can dip their pretzels in it. But remember— no double dipping!

Dump Cake

Georgia Lee Paul

1 package of white cake mix
2 cans of pie filling (blueberry, strawberry, or cherry)
2 Tbsp. butter or margarine cut into thin slices
Sliced almonds

Preheat oven to 350°.

In an 8 x 12 inch baking dish, put the cans of pie filling.

Dump the cake mix over the filling.

Place butter slices on top of cake mix.

Sprinkle almonds over all.

Bake for 40 minutes or until the top becomes light brown.

Lifestyle Evangelism

Cindy Schaefer

Matthew invited Jesus and his disciples to be his dinner guests, along with his fellow tax collectors and many other notorious sinners. The Pharisees were indignant. "Why does your teacher eat with such scum?" they asked his disciples. When he heard this, Jesus replied, "Healthy people don't need a doctor—sick people do."

—Matthew 9:10–12 NLT

One of the best ways to win people to the Lord is by living out your day-to-day life in front of them. Unfortunately, in trying to live "pure" lives, a lot of Christians have isolated themselves into little cloistered groups, where they only talk to or spend time with other Christians. This is a mistake Jesus never made.

Jesus doesn't ask us to compromise our values, but He did set a powerful example of befriending people whom the religious leaders of His day considered unworthy of His time. As you go through your day, make a point to open up your eyes to those around you who may not know Christ. Invite that less-than-desirable teacher to have lunch with you. Take your partying next-door neighbor a loaf of banana bread. Give that rebellious student some extra attention, maybe a special project or two.

Yes, it's risky. Some may look at you the way the Pharisees looked at Jesus, like you've lost your mind. But people respond to love. And when you love others genuinely and take an interest in their lives, you may find yourself in a position of leading some of them to the true source of all love, God himself.

make **your** day count

Instead of eating lunch in your classroom or hanging out with other
believers in the teachers' lounge, make it a point to have
lunch with that teacher whom others find difficult to love.
Or take a box of donuts to that teacher's class "just because."

Beyond Compare

Nancy C. Anderson

They are only comparing themselves with each other, and measuring themselves by themselves. What foolishness!
—2 Corinthians 10:12 NLT

I wished I had been as pretty as Juli or as funny as Chelsea. I wished I had been as smart as Jessica. I also envied Sandy, who lived in an oceanfront home, drove a $40,000 car, and wore a three-carat wedding ring. I was constantly comparing myself to others and never measuring up.

I thought, *Their lives seem so wonderful, and mine is so ordinary. I wish I could be more like them.* So I decided to ask them about their "perfect" lives. Upon closer examination, I found that these women were comparing themselves to others too!

Juli wished that she was tall like I am. Chelsea tried to make people laugh to keep up with her funny sister. Jessica said that she earned her master's degree just to please her father. And Sandy told me that she was lonely because her husband worked every weekend, and she wished she could trade her life of luxury for a husband who would go to church with her, like mine does. That's when I decided to stop comparing myself to others and instead, be thankful for the many blessings I have.

Most likely your students—who are trying to find their place in the world—are also wrestling with this issue. Regardless of one's age, financial status, race, or background, there will always be someone better than we are in a given area. As a teacher, you have an awesome opportunity to help your students avoid the self-defeating practice of comparing themselves to others by helping them to recognize and celebrate their own uniqueness.

make **your** day count

Make a list of the wonderful things and people in your life, and have your students do the same. Then talk to your students about being thankful as each of you begins to appreciate your lives for what they are, instead of bemoaning what they're not.

time **saving** tips

Resolving Classroom Conflict

Unfortunately, conflicts are inevitable. By teaching your students to resolve their conflicts in a healthy manner, you are equipping them with a vital life skill they can use into adulthood.

Teach your students to resolve their conflicts:

First separate the offenders until they can cool off. Then have them write down five things they admire about the other person. They are to stay in class until they can read their lists sincerely and offer a handshake or hug. Of course, this works for older students, but the principle can be applied to even kindergartners.

Don't allow students to speak unkindly of other students or teachers:

Invite violators to stand before the class and say five nice things about the person they have bad-mouthed.

Provide energy breaks:

If a student is disruptive and having a hard time paying attention due to an abundance of energy, have the student stand and for a full minute, tell a joke, sing a song, or do a silly dance. When the minute is up, have the student return to his or her desk and give you and their studies their full attention for the rest of the period.

easy **recipes**

Chocolate No-Bake Cookies[15]

2 cups sugar
$\frac{1}{2}$ cup milk
4 Tbsp. dry cocoa mix
$\frac{1}{2}$ tsp. salt
1 stick butter ($\frac{1}{2}$ cup)
$\frac{1}{4}$– $\frac{1}{2}$ cup peanut butter (optional)
2 tsp. vanilla
3 cups uncooked quick-cooking oats

Mix sugar, milk, cocoa, salt, and butter.

Bring to highest boil.

Boil one minute and remove from heat.

Add peanut butter, vanilla, and dry oats. Mix well.

Drop by the spoonful onto waxed paper.

time **saving** tips

Positive Strategies to Handle Difficult Students

Every teacher has war stories about problematic students. Develop strategies to turn difficult situations around.

Publicly verbalize the student's positive attributes:

You may be the only person to offer encouraging words to him or her.

Assign "important" responsibilities:

Giving the student an opportunity to excel in something and to receive positive feedback will help satisfy the need to act out for negative attention.

Document, document, document:

Document everything from what actions you take with the student to making copies of notes you send home to parents. You can never be too careful, and documentation could protect you from greater challenges down the road.

Establish a pre-assigned isolation area:

Make this a place near you to which a disorderly student may be directed. This will help to minimize the problem without taking too much time away from instruction.

Get to the root of the problem:

There is always a reason that a student acts out. Attempt to find the source of the problem as quickly as possible, and strive to eliminate or relieve it. The student's cry for negative attention could be a signal of a deeper issue. Keep an eye out for abuse or problems at home.

Raw Vegetable Salad[16]

5 cups broccoli, cut into bite-sized pieces
5 cups cauliflower, cut into bite-sized pieces
2 cups cheddar cheese, shredded
$2/3$ cup onion, chopped
$1/2$ cup raisins
$1/4$ cup sunflower seeds

Dressing:

1 cup mayonnaise
$1/2$ cup sugar or natural sugar substitute
2 Tbsp. apple cider vinegar

Combine all vegetables in a large bowl.

Mix dressing and pour over vegetables.

Toss well.

A Teacher's Prayer

Kim Lutherbeck

This is the confidence that we have in Him, that if we ask
anything according to His will, He hears us. And if we
know that He hears us, whatever we ask, we know that
we have the petitions that we have asked of Him.

—1 John 5:14,15 NKJV

Grant me the things that I will need
To do my job and always succeed.
Help me to know what to do and to say
To help those few students who refuse to obey.
Teach me how to love every child
Those who are busy and those who are mild.
Show me the gifts you've placed in each one
Help me to mold them to be like Your Son.
Give me Your eyes to see all their fears
Give me the words to bring them good cheer.
Make me Your servant and help me to serve
Allow me to give them all they deserve.
Keep my heart humble in all that I do
And help me to teach them to be just like You.
Thank you for caring and hearing my prayer.
And thank You for always being right there.

make **your** day count

As you pray this prayer today, rest in the fact that when you pray
for things that are in line with God's will—such as those things
in the petitions above—God delights in answering you.
He hears you when you call! Rejoice in that fact!

Because of Love

Holly Sonnenschein

Yet, O LORD, you are our Father.
We are the clay, you are the potter;
we are all the work of your hand.
—Isaiah 64:8

The rewards from teaching are endless. Many might question why someone would dedicate his or her life to teaching hundreds of school-aged children, but the answer is simple—because of love. There are many careers to choose from, but from how many could you walk away feeling as fulfilled—knowing that what you did, what you said, and how you said it changed a life?

Teaching is more than just filling minds with facts and ideas. It is more than grading a never-ending mountain of papers. It is more than just correcting misbehavior. It is allowing God to use you to speak words of life into young people.

God is the potter and we, His children, are the clay. He molds and shapes us to make us more like Him. As teachers, what we do and say to young people makes a similar impression. We have the opportunity to build up one who is down, to put a smile on the face of one who is hurting. We have the power to take students with low self-esteem and help them discover their infinite value.

Every day when we walk into the classroom, we need to remember that God has entrusted our students to us. We need to pray that we will see them the way that He sees them and that we will be sensitive to their needs. Then, because God has put us in a position to influence them, we must pray that God will empower us to make a difference.

You may never know the affect that your words have on a particular child, but that child will walk away knowing that he or she is a treasure.

make **your** day count

Before any of your students arrive this morning, pray that you will make today count in their lives. Pray that the Potter will work through you to mold their young lives for greatness.

time **saving** tips

Journaling

Shanna D. Gregor

Many find journaling to be an effective way to share their thoughts with God and to record those things they sense God is saying to them. It's also effective in putting things into perspective when dealing with life's challenges and emotional issues with others. Getting one's feelings down on paper often has a cathartic effect.

A journal doesn't have to be grammatically correct, and it doesn't have to be written in a notebook. Maybe speaking into a tape recorder or typing your thoughts on your computer suite you better.

Some questions to help you get started could include:

 Today is special because…

 Today I am thankful for…

 A Scripture I want to think about today is…

 Some questions I'd like God to answer are…

 Today I'm feeling…

easy **recipes**

Super Spud

Baked potato
Cottage cheese
Cheddar cheese, grated
Tomato, chopped
Green onions chopped
Black olives, sliced or chopped
Salt and pepper
Any other toppings that appeal to you

Bake potato by method you like best.

After it is baked, use a knife to cut the potato open lengthwise, but do not cut in two. Lay open the potato so that insides face up, and slightly mash. (Leave skins on for optimum nutrition.)

Spread a layer of cottage cheese over the potato, then a layer of cheese.

Continue layering other ingredients according to your taste.

Voilà! Dinner is served.

Today Is a Gift

Shanna D. Gregor

[Jesus said,] "Give your entire attention to what God is doing right now."
—Matthew 6:34 MESSAGE

Classes, friends, parties, cheerleading, drama club, research papers, and an after-school job packed my high school years with what seemed to be endless activities. I pushed forward for tomorrow, in a hurry to grow up and pursue what I perceived to be real life.

Real life hit me in the face my senior year when I learned that my grandmother—a foundational stone in my spiritual life—was diagnosed with cancer. My world stood still the day she died. For the first time in a long time, I experienced today as only today.

I watched the sun come up the next morning. I didn't think about tomorrow or the next day. I was no longer in a hurry to discover my future. I realized that each day is a gift and every moment, filled with purpose. So I changed my focus. I began to fulfill God's purpose in my life each day and to enjoy each day as the gift it is.

Do you find yourself thinking, *Things will different when…* or *If only…* or *Tomorrow I'll…?* Are you waiting for tomorrow instead of making the most of today? Living in the present—

conscious of God, with a thankful heart—will help you experience your life's journey to the fullest today.

Consider passing this lesson on to your students as well. Then—today—enjoy the school day that you share together.

make **your** day count

Determine to live today—today. Live each moment in the present, drinking in the blessing of the moment and voicing your thanks to God. Enjoy today! It's God's gift to you.

time **saving** tips

Renewing Your Spirit

Darla Satterfield Davis

Teaching can become all-consuming. Sometimes you need a little something to lift your spirits and help you through those challenging days that come along.

On breaks read your Bible:

Keep a Bible on a classroom shelf, so you can turn to it for inspiration and to help revitalize your spirit for the remainder of the day.

Start the day with prayer:

Spending your first few waking minutes with God—asking for guidance, wisdom, and patience—is the best way to start your day off right. But don't stop there. Throughout the day, continue asking God for what you need and remember to thank Him for refreshing You with His presence.

Just for today, give your cares over to God:

It can be difficult to let go of everything and trust in God. Decide to step away from the concern for just one day. It will give you a break and recharge your batteries for the days ahead.

Superb Sweet Potato Pie

Lisa Anne Camille Louissaint

2 fairly large sweet potatoes
1 ⅓ cups granulated sugar
4 oz. butter softened
3 large eggs
½ cup canned condensed milk
¼ tsp. cinnamon
¼ tsp. ground cloves
½ tsp. nutmeg (I prefer freshly grated)
½ tsp. vanilla extract
1 9-inch, deep-dish pie crust (frozen works great)

Wrap sweet potatoes in foil and bake at 425° for 45 minutes.

When potatoes are cooled, peel and slice crosswise (to avoid strings).

Reduce oven heat to 375°.

Mash potatoes and add other ingredients.

Beat until well mixed and pour into pie shell.

Bake on a cookie sheet in the middle of the oven until middle is set (about 50–55 minutes). Cover edges with foil to prevent them from over browning.

Maple-Cinnamon Whipped Cream

1 cup heavy cream
1 tsp. granulated sugar
3 tsp. real maple syrup
½ tsp. cinnamon

Place beater and bowl in freezer while pie is baking.

When pie is cool, remove whipped cream ingredients from freezer and whip until stiff.

time **saving** tips

More Ways to Renew Your Spirit

Darla Satterfield Davis

Find some quiet time:

Sometimes it helps to have some silent alone time—away from shuffling papers and grinding pencil sharpeners. Your car may be the perfect place.

Eat lunch outside:

Of course you can't do this on days when the weather in inclement, but nothing lifts the spirits like enjoying the beauty of nature with its many sights and sounds.

Get away for a retreat or other function:

Break the routine of your life. Introduce some adventure into your world, as well as a change of scenery. It can be very energizing to meet new people who share common interests. You may even make a new friend or two!

Do an anonymous kind deed for someone:

It is indeed more blessed to give than receive. It fills your heart with joy.

easy **recipes**

Fruit Smoothies

2 oz. pineapple or apple juice
½ frozen banana (remove peel before freezing in a Ziploc bag)
4 pieces frozen fruit such as strawberries, peaches, or a handful
  of blueberries
2 Tbsp. honey
2 cups crushed ice

Whirl all ingredients in blender until smooth.

Believe the Report of the Lord

Lindsay Roberts

Abraham never wavered in believing God's promise....
He was absolutely convinced that God
was able to do anything he promised.

—Romans 4:20,21 NLT

What do you do when you get a bad report from the doctor or some other source? If a bad report says one thing but the Word of God says another, *you* decide which report you're going to believe. You can either believe the bad report, which may be a *fact*, or you can believe the *truth* in God's Word.

In Genesis 15:5, God told Abraham that he would become the father of many nations. He went on to say that Abraham would have a son and his descendants would be more numerous than the stars in the sky! Abraham was one hundred years old when God said this! Abraham's exceeding age was the *fact*, but fathering a child was *God's report!* And we know the outcome: God's promise came to pass.

If you have received a bad report, get into God's Word regarding your need, then choose to put your faith in that truth. If you find your faith wavering, be like the man who approached Jesus in Mark 9:24 NLT, saying, "I do believe, but help me not to doubt!" God will help you with any areas of unbelief.

Draw a line in the sand and stand on the promises in God's Word, then don't waver. Choose to believe the report of the Lord![17]

make **your** day count

If you have received a bad report that is a fact as far as this world is concerned, find a Bible promise regarding the situation. Then draw a line in the sand today and choose to believe the report of the Lord.

High School Heartbreak

Nancy C. Anderson

He heals the brokenhearted
and binds up their wounds.
—Psalm 147:3

I paced the floor of the high school cafeteria as I waited for my boyfriend, Jason. He was late for lunch, so I went looking for him. As I walked around the corner, I saw him— walking hand in hand with my best friend, Jill!

She had the decency to turn her head in shame, but he looked me in the eye, smiled a cruel smile, and casually said, "Hi Nance." They walked away, and I fell against the wall as my knees and heart folded.

He had been my whole world. I thought my life was over, and I felt less than worthless from the betrayal. He temporarily broke my heart, but I learned a valuable lesson as I watched him, a month later, break Jill's heart too. I asked the Lord to help me forgive him—and He did. I never again measured my worth by another person's loyalty, but learned instead to rely on God's consistent and unfailing love.

At some time and in some way, each of us has been hurt by another individual. Your students, too, may be experiencing the heartbreak of a boyfriend or girlfriend, their parents' divorce, or some other circumstance. As a teacher, you have the wisdom that years of experience affords, and your students may need someone to help them see the big picture. You have an invaluable opportunity to impart healing where there is hurt and love where this is pain.

Be sensitive to the emotional situations your students are going through. Offer them an open ear and words of encouragement, and steer them toward the freedom of forgiveness. And whether you can pray openly with them or not, you can ask God to impart His healing and grace.

make **your** day count

If there is anyone who has betrayed you, ask the Lord for the strength to forgive that person, so you can exchange the burden of bitterness for the freedom of forgiveness. And be on the lookout for those students who may be experiencing heartbreak and offer your support.

A Shining Example

Amanda Pilgrim

Set an example for the believers in speech,
in life, in love, in faith and in purity.
—1 Timothy 4:12

She never won any awards, nor was she highly acclaimed in her field, but Coach Harrison was my hero. She was strong and supportive, and she believed in me.

I began playing basketball in the seventh grade. I was awkward and had no idea what to do on the court, but Coach Harrison was there. She taught me the rules and the basics and instilled in me the love for athletics. She was there urging me on when I wanted to throw in the towel. She was there to support me when I was angry and hurt. She was there to push me to the next level when I refused to push myself.

Coach Harrison was more than just a coach; she was an example of what a teacher is supposed to be—someone to help you when you fall down, someone to challenge you to make it to the finish line, someone you can look up to and respect.

She never allowed us to play dirty, to take cheap shots, or to bad-mouth the other team. To her, it really was about *how* you played the game. Coach Harrison taught me many things over the years, but the most important ones were how to be a respectable person, to play fair, to play hard, and to give it

110 percent. She instilled these values in us not just to be used in the game of basketball, but also to apply in life.

I think of Coach Cheri Harrison as I coach my own basketball teams today. I try to inspire my teams as she inspired me, to challenge them to push themselves to be better people. I thank God for teachers like Coach Harrison. She showed me what it was to be a better person.

make **your** day count

Pick one trait that you would like to instill in your students today. Focus on that trait for one full day, and try to be a living example of it to your students. Keep in mind that your actions speak louder than your words.

time **saving** tips

The First Day of School

Amanda Pilgrim

The first day of school should be a time of fun and celebration! It will set the tone for the rest of the year.

Recruit new-student escorts:

New students usually struggle with the first few weeks of school. Having a returning student act as an ambassador to show the new students around the building, introduce them to people, and generally get them acquainted with the routine of the school can make adjustments less stressful.

Write a letter to each student:

Write a short but sincere letter of welcome to each student and place it on their desks along with a colorful pencil or eraser. Be sure to have extras on hand for those unexpected new students.

State your expectations up front:

Everyone works better when they know what is expected from them at the start. Go over the rules, systems, and your expectations for your class on the first day. Answering questions and sorting out any confusion will erase many unnecessary difficulties in the future. Consider asking the students what their expectations are of you. It can offer valuable insight that you might want to implement. This also helps the students feel that they are participating in the administration of their classroom.

easy **recipes**

Summer Squash Slaw

Abby Detcher

2 small yellow summer squash, julienned
2 small zucchini, julienned
1 small sweet red pepper, julienned
$\frac{1}{3}$ cup sliced onion
3 Tbsp. vegetable oil
2 Tbsp. cider or white wine vinegar
1 Tbsp. mayonnaise
1 tsp. sugar
$\frac{1}{2}$ tsp. dill weed
$\frac{1}{2}$ tsp. garlic salt
$\frac{1}{4}$ tsp. celery salt
$\frac{1}{4}$ tsp. pepper

In a large bowl, combine squash, zucchini, red pepper, and onion.

In a small bowl, combine remaining ingredients; mix well.

Pour over squash mixture and toss to coat.

Cover and refrigerate.

Serve with slotted spoon.

My Peace I Give You

Lindsay Roberts

[Jesus said,] "Peace I leave with you; my peace I give you.
I do not give to you as the world gives. Do not let
your hearts be troubled and do not be afraid."
—John 14:27

Right now, people everywhere are scared to death of what the future holds because of the events of September 11. The world is in chaos and people are looking for a safety net. Many are facing circumstances never seen before and wondering where to turn for answers.

But we have to remember that when the twin towers in New York City came down, Jesus didn't fall off His throne. God didn't shake in His boots. He is still sovereign! And He's saying to us, *Call upon Me. Listen to Me. Don't worry. I am with you. Don't be afraid.* His Word reassures us in John 14:27 that Jesus left us His peace. God is here to help us!

When the world situation looks dark as it did that horrendous day, how much brighter the light of our salvation shines! And yes, it's possible that things might get even darker, but when your mouth, your heart, and your spirit bless the Lord, you can be filled with the peace of God that surpasses all human understanding, no matter what is going on around you. (Phil. 4:7.) God wants to calm your fears and bring you peace and strength in times of crisis.

And this peace is not for you alone. Each day you are surrounded by young people who look to you for guidance and support. If you are anxious and full of fear, you will not have the resources to calm the fears of your students. But when you are resting in the Lord and His peace is within you, then you will be able to pass this peace on to your students and anyone else you come into contact with.[18]

make **your** day count

Jesus left you His peace, a peace not affected by what is going on in the world. Read Psalm 91, and whenever you feel worried or afraid today, go to your heavenly Father, rest in His arms, and soak up His boundless peace.

"Teacher, Teacher, Teacher!"

Stephanie Carlile Murrill

We also have joy with our troubles, because we know
that these troubles produce patience. And patience
produces character, and character produces hope.
And this hope will never disappoint us, because
God has poured out his love to fill our hearts.

—Romans 5:3–5 NCV

We have all had one. You know—*that* student. The one who—no matter how many times you repeat things in front of the class—comes tapping on your arm. "Teacher, how do we do this?" "Teacher, what page do we do?" "Teacher, do we have to write this in cursive?"

For me, students who wouldn't listen had been one of the most frustrating parts of teaching. I tried everything to combat the problem. I wrote announcements on the board. I wrote notes. I made the students write notes. Nothing worked, and I found myself getting easily agitated.

One night, after a very trying day, I began to pray. I was impressed to open my Bible and through hot tears happened upon Romans 5. "We also have joy with our troubles, because we know that these troubles produce patience." I had never thought about finding joy in the midst of my frustration.

I also began to realize how often I mess up and go to Christ for forgiveness and reassurance. He never gets agitated with me. His patience and forgiveness is always abounding. I quickly realized that I had a lot of changing to do.

I started the next day with a new resolve. When I encountered my usual problem, I didn't get upset. I smiled and calmly explained the answer. As my attitude changed, I noticed that my students' attitudes began to change. I also noticed the listening problem was getting better.

Let God turn an otherwise frustrating situation into a joyful one. Not only will your stress be lightened, it will change the whole atmosphere in your classroom.

make **your** day count

Today, when things might not go as planned, don't get frustrated—
be joyful. Make a joke, laugh, enjoy yourself. It will not only
make you feel better, but your whole class will benefit.

time **saving** tips

"What Do I Do Next?"

Stephanie Carlile Murrill

Create a "What Do I Do Next?" poster for students who consistently get their work done early. Include a large list of things they could do such as read a book, write a skit or play, spend time on the computer, study for an upcoming test, draw a picture, make a card for someone, make up a new game, practice spelling words, and anything else you can think of.

You might also consider giving small, token prizes or using some other reward system for those students who make good use of their extra time.

Sunshine Slaw[19]

4 cups cabbage, shredded
1 cup crushed pineapple, drained
1 cup mandarin oranges (or freshly sliced)
$\frac{1}{2}$ cup celery, diced
1 cup mayonnaise
$\frac{1}{4}$ cup nonfat sour cream
2 Tbsp. fruit juice
2 Tbsp. white vinegar
1 Tbsp. sugar or natural sugar substitute
Dash of salt

Mix well.

Refrigerate for several hours.

time **saving** tips

Make It Come Alive

Linda Burritt

When teaching middle school social studies and geography, I have found that it is very effective to read books to the students that relate to the area and people group we are studying. My favorite is when we read the condensed version of *Robinson Crusoe* as we are learning about European—especially English—culture. One of our exercises is to determine the latitude and longitude of the location where the shipwreck was to have taken place.

We also study comparison charts, do research papers, and even biographical reports on the author and others who have written similar stories. I try to cover all angles of each people group and geographic area so that the material will come alive and have a lasting effect on the students.

Italian Meatloaf

1 lb. ground beef or turkey
1 egg, slightly beaten
$^1/_2$ tsp. salt
$^1/_4$ tsp. pepper
1 Tbsp. Italian seasoning
1–2 cloves garlic, minced
1 cup Pepperidge Farm Herb Seasoned Stuffing
1 small onion, chopped fine
1 carrot, grated fine
$^1/_2$ cup finely chopped bell pepper
2 cups Prego spaghetti sauce, or enough to cover loaf
Grated parmesan cheese (not the kind in the can)

In large mixing bowl, beat egg and add salt, pepper, Italian seasoning, and garlic. Mix well.

Add stuffing, onion, carrot, and bell pepper. Mix well.

Add meat.

Using your hands, mix all ingredients well.

Place in a greased loaf pan and pour spaghetti sauce over all.

Top with parmesan cheese.

Cook at 350° for 45 minutes to an hour, until center is firm.

Loaf pan will fit inside many toaster ovens, and the meatloaf can be cooked in it instead of heating up the regular oven.

All Aboard!

Tonya Hudson

Let your eyes look straight ahead,
And your eyelids look right before you.
Ponder the path of your feet,
And let your ways be established.
Do not turn to the right or the left.

—Proverbs 4:25–27 NKJV

As a teacher, I know the importance of focus. When I first began teaching, there were some days that would start out as hopeful new beginnings but then crumble before my eyes into piles of distracting interruptions, unfinished lessons, and frustrated sighs. They were days that left me wondering what, if anything, my students had gained from their encounter with me.

One morning during prayer, God began to show me a picture of *focus* as being a train track, with my daily purpose as my appointed destination. He showed me that though my "train" may encounter frequent stops and unforeseen delays, as long as it continued on its track, it would arrive as intended.

I began to see that even when my "passengers" grew restless and weary, I could alter my approach without abandoning my purpose for each lesson and project. This has allowed me to relax into flexibility without falling into fruitlessness.

Equally as important, I've learned to tailor every word, every instruction, and even every correction to fit into my daily focus. I marvel at the number of opportunities God supplies during classroom routine to reinforce whatever I am teaching. I've come to understand that even the interruptions can be used for instruction.

With these insights, my teaching has taken on new meaning, and yours can too! Let God-given, daily focus guide you (and your students) to your destination today.

make **your** day count

Take a moment right now to ask God what is the one, most important thing you should impart to your students today. Then, let His answer guide you in all that you teach, say, and do in your classroom.

Swimming Upstream

Cindy Schaefer

*The sinful nature desires what is contrary to the
Spirit, and the Spirit what is contrary to the sinful
nature. They are in conflict with each other,
so that you do not do what you want.*
—Galatians 5:17

Not long ago, I was at the mall on a busy Saturday. The
stores were packed, and the lines were several people deep. I
stopped to rest my shopping-weary feet near the main mall
escalator. It was there that I saw a very brave young boy
attempt to go up the escalator—the *down* escalator! He
managed to make it to the top, but not without colliding
with a few dozen brim-full shopping bags and collecting
more than a few dirty looks.

If you've been a Christian for long, you may be able to
identify with this young boy. Do you ever get the feeling that
you're trying to swim upstream when it would be easier to go
with the flow? If so, good! Romans 12:2 says, "Do not
conform any longer to the pattern of this world, but be trans-
formed by the renewing of your mind." Though the entire
world operates on natural law, with its consequences of sin
and death, we as followers of Christ should live our lives
according to biblical principles, ruled by the law of the Spirit,
which brings life. (Rom. 8:2.)

When people enter a covenant relationship with Jesus, they break the old tie that bound them to sin and enter a new relationship of life in Christ. Don't be discouraged as you walk out your new life. You may get a few dirty looks as you walk the way that is opposite to that of the crowd, but the end result will be worth all the effort!

make **your** day count

Is there an area where you have previously gone with the flow, but now God is dealing with you about swimming upstream? Call on a Christian friend who can pray with you and offer support. In class today, talk to your students about taking a stand and doing the right thing.

Being Led by the Spirit of God

Patty Staley

Those who are led by the Spirit of God are sons of God.
—Romans 8:14

Joey was ten and had just gone through the pain of his parents' divorce, their remarriages, and then a move. He was not about to give me a chance to prove to him that he could like me or school. He would slouch, mock me, and angrily glare at me. I needed God's wisdom to handle this one.

When praying, I felt that the Lord was instructing me to *ignore* Joey! That was the exact opposite of what I in my humanness wanted to do, but I obeyed. I didn't react to his attitudes. I didn't correct them. I didn't even acknowledge them!

I work in a Christian school, and one day I was walking through the classroom praying over my students. When I came to Joey, a deep sadness welled up within me, so much so that it brought tears to my eyes. The Holy Spirit gave me insight into the intense pain this child was experiencing.

I took Joey aside, hugged him, and quietly told him that God understood what he was going through. I even shared some ways that I had been hurt as a child and how God helped me love those who had mistreated me. I went on to tell him that God helped me overcome the rejection I had suffered and He brought healing to the wounds caused by harsh words.

As I spoke these words, which I believe the Holy Spirit was leading me to say, Joey finally broke. He gave his heart to the Lord that day, and what a transformation took place! He became my best student and the most joyful boy in the class!

God's ways really are higher than ours, and when we follow them, the results are miraculous. (Isa. 55:8.)

make **your** day count

Ask God to lead you by His Spirit in the way you are to handle difficult situations with your students today. Your wisdom won't change things, but God's will. And His wisdom and His ways are so much higher and better than our own.

time **saving** tips

Making Everlasting Christmas Wreaths

Patty Staley

This wreath looks beautiful and will last a lifetime. My daughter made one for her grandmother ten years ago; her grandmother still uses it, and it still looks great.

You will need a wire coat hanger and a white trash bag.

 Mold the coat hanger into a circle.

 Cut the trash bag into 6-inch strips, 1 inch wide.

 Tie each of these around the wire, pushing the pieces together until the entire circle is filled.

 Put a red bow at the top and decorate with small colorful ornaments.

Rice Almondine

Janet A. Nation

1 stick butter
1 cup raw rice (not instant)
1 can French onion soup
1 can beef consommé
$\frac{1}{2}$ cup sliced almonds

Melt butter in 9 x 13 inch casserole dish and spread around to coat the bottom and sides.

Put remaining ingredients into the casserole dish.

Bake for 45–46 minutes at 350°.

Christmas in China

Janet A. Nation

For unto us a Child is born,
Unto us a Son is given.
—Isaiah 9:6 NKJV

In the fall of 1997, my husband, Galen, and I moved to Wuhan, China, where I taught English as a second language and Galen taught engineering courses to university students there. Because of the relationships that we formed with the students, we had many opportunities to share the Gospel.

As the Christmas holidays approached, we prayed for creative ways to share the true message surrounding Christmas and the birth of Christ. As we scoured bookstores all over the city—Wuhan has a population of 7.3 million people—we found only *one* card that depicted the familiar nativity scene with baby Jesus in a manger! Instead, Santa Claus faces hung in most store windows. It was apparent that the only concept that had been grasped from our Western culture was that of the *commercial* Christmas.

Accepting an invitation to be the entertainment for a student-body Christmas party, we spent time seeking the Lord as to what to share. Arriving early, we walked in to find disco music blaring, strobe lights gyrating, wine overflowing, and students wearing Mardi Gras style masks! In the center of the room stood a forlorn-looking "Charlie Brown" type

Christmas tree. Needless to say, the students' rendition of Christmas was not at all what we had expected.

Suddenly the lights went out due to a power outage, and we stood in total darkness. Asking for candles, we were handed a plentiful supply. My husband and I began to sing "Silent Night," and a reverent hush fell over the crowd. As we shared the age-old story of Christ's birth, inebriated students sobered up, and tears flowed unashamedly. We told them that God loved each of them and that His love had brought us to China. Truly, Jesus became the entertainment that night, and no longer was Christmas just a "Western thing"!

make **your** day count

Pray for creative ways to share the message of Jesus Christ with your students as well as your coworkers, friends, and neighbors. Pray that God will prepare their hearts to be open when the time is right. You don't have to do this alone. God will help you.

A Passion for the Nations

Kim Lutherbeck

*[Jesus said,] "This Gospel of the kingdom will
be preached in the whole world as a testimony
to all nations, and then the end will come."*
—Matthew 24:14

As a Pre-K teacher in a Christian school, I believe it is
important for me to teach my young students to think
beyond themselves and their immediate world and help
them develop a heart for the nations. During my second year
of teaching, God showed me a creative way to do this. Each
week we review a letter of the alphabet; and I choose two
nations that begin with that letter, and we pray for them.

You might not have the liberty to pray in class, but you
can teach on various nations as part of social studies and
geography classes and develop in your students an appreciation for the people in those countries. You can bring it down
to the human level so that your students realize you are dis-
cussing real people, just like them. Depending on the ages of
your students, you might even consider having your class
adopt a pen pal from another country.

The idea I believe God gave me is so simple, but the
results have been incredible. The children in my class have a
genuine passion for the people of the world. I never have to
beg any of them to pray because they are quick to volunteer.

The parents of these children are in awe over the excitement that their little ones have for the world. At home the children are praying for the nations when they are saying their bedtime prayers and blessing their food.

It is important to remember that the children I teach are four and five. But if they can get a passion for the nations at this young age, imagine what will happen as they get older. I am raising up world changers!

make **your** day count

Make you day count! Pick a nation and study what life is like for the people who live there. Perhaps consider having your class adopt a pen pal from that country. If you have the freedom to do so, pray for that nation as a class.

time **saving** tips

Setting the Standard

Raise the bar at your school and in your classroom. Teaching is a profession that deserves respect and admiration. Be deserving of both.

Dress professionally:
Students and others will relate to you according to how you carry yourself and the manner in which you dress.

Make eye contact and really listen:
Just as you expect to have the full attention of your class, be sure to set the example and give them that same respect in your dealings with them.

Exercise good manners:
Using phrases such as "Thank you," "You're welcome," and "Please" establishes a courteous atmosphere and sets the example for your students to follow. Proper etiquette reflects a respect for others, and it is a life skill that will benefit your students long after they leave the walls of your classroom.

Be an encourager:
Listening to and encouraging your students will go a long way in building self-esteem and a sense of personal worth. You may be the only person to give your students positive feedback on a given day.

Praise publicly, reprimand privately:
Praising your students publicly will instill a positive self-image, and by reprimanding in private, you preserve the students' dignity and prevent the damaging effects of humiliation.

Sausage Squares

1 lb. hot (spicy) sausage
Cheddar cheese, shredded
1 cup milk
1 cup Bisquick
6 eggs

Sauté sausage, drain thoroughly, and place in bottom of a greased, 8-inch square pan or casserole dish.

Cover with generous portion of cheese.

Mix milk, Bisquick, and eggs thoroughly, and pour over ingredients in pan.

Bake at 375° for 30 minutes or until set.

Freezes well.

time **saving** tips

More Ways to Set the Standard

Don't engage in teachers' lounge gossip:

Although the lounge can be a source of creative ideas and inspiration, it can also be a breeding ground for negativity. Gossip only serves to hurt and offend others. If gossip is plaguing your lounge, save yourself the mental energy and walk away.

Refrain from interrupting students:

By doing this, you show your students the same respect you expect them to exhibit towards you. Wait until they are finished speaking before interjecting any comments or questions.

Never leave the classroom unsupervised:

Too many accidents can happen when a teacher leaves the room. Send a reliable student to find an adult to watch your class while you step out for a few minutes.

Have business cards available:

Not only will this reflect professionalism on your part, it will enable parents to get in touch with you quickly and as needed. Include the contact information of your choice, such as your home telephone number, cell phone number, and e-mail address. With a computer, you can even make your own business cards, using precut card stock made for that purpose.

easy **recipes**

Texas Quiche

One 4-oz. can green chilies

12 eggs

2 lb. cheddar cheese

Cut up green chilies in blender.

Pour in eggs and cheddar cheese. *Briefly* blend ingredients. (Eggs will get foamy if blended too long.)

Pour into greased 9 x 13-inch casserole dish.

Bake at 350° for 30 minutes or until knife inserted in center comes out clean.

Passing the Stress Test

Lindsay Roberts

Count it all joy when you fall into various trials, knowing that the testing of your faith produces patience. But let patience have its perfect work, that you may be perfect and complete, lacking nothing. If any of you lacks wisdom, let him ask of God…and it will be given to him.

—James 1:2–5 NKJV

Are you under enormous pressure? God has not called you to be stressed, frustrated, or upset. Let's look at what the Word of God says regarding things you can do to take control of stress and pass the stress test.

First, count it all joy. You do it because you know this: that the trying of your faith works patience, and when patience has had its perfect work, you will be left wanting nothing! I believe that when we count it all joy, it causes God to come on the scene and Satan to go the other direction.

Second, remember that God is working in you. Let patience have her perfect work. Most people think patience is waiting and doing nothing until something happens. Not true! *Patience* means hopeful endurance, tolerance, diligence, self-possessed waiting, and dogged tenacity.

Third, ask for wisdom. Notice that we do the asking and God does the answering.

There are many great Scriptures to help you deal with stress, but until you apply them, they might as well be fairy dust to you. It's time to decide, "I will not react to stress and fall apart, but I will respond with the Word of God!" Choosing the right attitude in the middle of stress can bring the answers from the Lord.[20]

make **your** day count

In whatever stressful situation you find yourself today, run to the shelter of God's Word. Read God's promises regarding your situation out loud. Hearing yourself speak God's promises will help to build your faith and keep stress at bay.

A Little One-on-One

Shanna D. Gregor

"Here I am! I stand at the door and knock.
If anyone hears my voice and opens the door,
I will come in and eat with him, and he with me."

—Revelation 3:20

As a teacher, have you found that through your students you learn much about yourself? That is how it is for me as a mother.

When my children were small and I needed to tell them something important—like "Stay out of the street," "Don't stick your hand in the VCR, anymore," or "We don't play with kitchen knives,"—I would put my hands on their little faces and turn their eyes toward mine. I would then ask them to tell me what I had said. That way I knew they had heard and clearly understood my instruction.

After one of my one-on-one conversations with my youngest son, I took a step back and smiled to myself as I watched him bounce on his merry way. Then the thought occurred to me, *Does God ever want to pull my face near His for a little one-on-one?* In my heart, I knew the answer was a resounding yes.

The activities of life can fill up every space of my day. Exhausted and ready to rest, I often realize I've not communicated with the most important person in my life—my heavenly Father.

Time for oneself is often a luxury in our fast-paced lives. Just as you relish your few moments alone, remember God wants time with you. He has much to impart into your life and heart. Give Him a little one-on-one.

make **your** day count

When you think of the heavenly Father, know that He's thinking of you.
The very moment you think of Him, take that moment to breathe
a prayer of thanks. Then listen. He has instructions for you today.

Forgiven

Amanda Pilgrim

Do you despise the riches of His goodness,
forbearance, and longsuffering, not knowing
that the goodness of God leads you to repentance?
—Romans 2:4 NKJV

I tried to read his expression as anger twisted my insides. He sat stone still, glaring at me.

"How *could* you have stolen the grade book?" I demanded.

No answer.

I wanted to impose a punishment that he wouldn't forget, but I sensed God wanted me to handle this a different way. I could see right through Jared's hollow defiance and was reminded of the many times I had failed. No matter how many times I had blown it, each time God had picked me up and forgiven me. I imagined myself sitting in Jared's chair, fearful of what punishment lay in store for my misdeeds.

I slowly sat down in front of him and said, "I forgive you."

"What?" came his surprised reply.

"I forgive you," I said again.

"What are you going to do to me?" he asked shakily.

"Absolutely nothing. You are free to go."

He looked at me bewildered. "But I stole a grade book. Aren't you going to punish me?"

"Not this time. I am giving you an absolute pardon if you would like it."

He stared at me for a moment, then his eyes filled with tears. "Mrs. Pilgrim, I'm so sorry. I didn't want to steal the book, but the other boys were making fun of me."

"I understand peer pressure can be very difficult to handle," I said. "And I forgive you, but I ask that you never do anything like that again, okay?"

"I promise, Mrs. Pilgrim, never."

That day I learned an invaluable lesson—to look at my students the way God looks at us—individually. I learned not to react out of emotion, but to listen to God's Spirit within me, allowing Him to guide my actions. He knows the key to unlock every heart.

make **your** day count

As you deal with your challenging students today, ask God how to handle each individual case. God knows the heart of every student, and He can lead you in the way that will be most effective when dealing with each of them.

time **saving** tips

Teaching Beginning Readers

Linda Jordan & Linda Burritt

Learning to read is one of the foundational skills that children will build upon for the rest of their lives. The following are tips that have proven effective in teaching young readers.

When introducing special sounds, the teacher can use her fingers on one hand to signal how many letters are in each sound and on the other hand, how many letters are in the complete word. For example, if working on the blend *STR,* the teacher holds up three fingers on the right hand. Then, to form the word *STRAP,* the teacher holds up five fingers on the left. This helps the students visualize the special sounds and words.

Sound, blend, and pronounce every word, then have the students write the complete word on individual dry-erase boards.

Word-family books are a type of flip chart tool that can be used to teach blends and consonants to beginning readers. If working on the *AT* ending, for example, write out the word *BAT* in large, bold letters. On each of the other pages, half the size of the initial page, write a consonant that can be used with the *AT* ending to form words like *CAT, HAT, PAT, SLAT, MAT* and so on. In this example, the half pages containing the beginning consonants are attached to the top left of the full page and can be flipped down over the *B* to form the other words.

World's Easiest Cobbler

1 stick butter or margarine
1 cup sugar
1 cup flour
3 tsp. baking powder
1 cup milk
1 can sliced peaches in light syrup (remove 2 Tbsp. of juice)
Vanilla ice cream

Melt butter in 1 ½ -quart baking dish. Roll dish around so that all sides and the bottom are coated.

Mix dry ingredients and pour over butter. Do not stir.

Pour milk, peaches, and juice (minus the 2 Tbsp.) over dry ingredients. Do not stir.

Cook uncovered at 375° for at least 35 minutes until nicely browned and bubbling.

Let cool for a few minutes, but while still warm, serve in a bowl with a scoop of vanilla ice cream on top.

Can substitute a can of blueberries, blackberries, or any other canned fruit for peaches.

Face Your Fear

Nancy C. Anderson

Whenever I am afraid, I will trust in You.

—Psalm 56:3 NKJV

When I was in the tenth grade, I was painfully shy. I walked through the halls with my head down and my arms tightly crossed. I was afraid of rejection, so I never took any risks, but I was always lonely.

One day I saw a poster announcing tryouts for the school musical. I had always had a secret dream to be onstage, so I faced my fear of rejection and prayed for the Lord to give me courage and a strong voice as I auditioned.

I was amazed when they gave me the part of "Townswoman #3." I didn't have any lines, but I was thrilled to sing and dance in the chorus. The rehearsals were a lot of fun, and it was great to discover the wonderful feeling of being part of a group with a common goal. I even made several new friends to hang out with, and I began walking the halls with a confident smile and my head held high.

My shyness and fear almost kept me from that wonderful experience. But because I took the steps to go beyond my comfort zone, the Lord made a way for me to write and perform in thirty-five drama productions for a Christian theater.

Many of your students feel just as I did, and without some encouragement from an outside source, many will stay trapped in their loneliness and fear. Look for those students who don't seem to fit in and are lonely. Find out what their interests are and help them get plugged into an area of school where they can experience a whole new way of life.

make **your** day count

Take a small step toward a larger goal. If you are afraid or confused about where to start, ask the Lord for His guidance and then break the goal down into tiny steps. Then, slowly, one at a time, walk up those stairs. You will be amazed at the heights you will reach!

Take Charge of Stress

Lindsay Roberts

The LORD gives strength to his people;
the LORD blesses his people with peace.
—Psalm 29:11

When my daughter, Chloe, was seven, she entered her first horse-riding competition on a thirty-year-old Arabian horse, whom she was only going to trot around the arena. As proud parents, we were watching from the stands. When they reached the center of the arena, however, it was as if the horse realized he was an Arabian. He began cantering like a crazy horse, then took off like a rocket with Chloe bouncing to high heaven.

My husband, Richard, and I were terrified beyond words and began praying. Meanwhile Chloe was screaming at the top of her lungs, while the horse just ignored her and headed for one of the exits. Then, instead of stopping, the horse kept going and ran out of the arena!

Richard and I quickly made our way out of the stands and ran out of the building after them. By the time we caught up with her, we could see she had burst into tears. There was no applause, no ribbon. Nothing but humiliation.

Then to our surprise, Chloe grabbed the horse by the bit, jerked his face to hers, looked him straight in the eyes, and said, "Why did you embarrass me like that in front of all those people? Don't you *ever* do that to me again!"

Somehow she was able to draw from deep within, from that place of inner strength placed there by God Himself.

The lesson? When you react, stress controls you. When you respond with God's deposit deep within you, you take control over stress. If a seven-year-old can do it, we can too![21]

make **your** day count

More than likely, stress will come your way today. Ask for God's peace to fill you so that instead of reacting and allowing the stress to control you, you can respond with God's peace and seize the day.

time **saving** tips

Grading Made Easy

With enormous amounts of papers to grade, shortcuts and simple ideas to help with the grading process can keep things flowing smoothly.

Institute and utilize answer columns:

Having your students make answer columns on one side of their papers can make grading easier and faster for you. These columns are convenient for you to check—even multiple papers at a time—and if there is a question, you have the original problem right there to double-check.

Assign student numbers:

Giving students classroom numbers at the beginning of the year can make several processes flow easier. Have students put their number at the top of all their papers, so you can quickly check and see if someone did not turn in work. The students can also walk in numerical order or reverse numerical order to recess and lunch. In addition, all textbooks can be marked with the student numbers, and you will know right away who is responsible for any books that might be missing during inventory.

Combine assignments:

To cut down on the number of pages to correct, try combining assignments. For example, spelling or vocabulary words can be used in a language arts essay. If the spelling words are underlined, you can check them quickly and then read the essay. Then record both grades in the corresponding subjects.

Cheesy Spinach and Rice

1 ½ cups raw rice (brown or white)
½ stick butter
1 cup chopped green onions
1 can cream of chicken soup
1 package frozen, chopped spinach, thawed.
2 cups cheddar cheese, shredded
1 egg, beaten
Salt and pepper to taste.

Cook rice according to package directions.

Put spinach in strainer and press out water.

Mix all ingredients together and put into greased 9 x 13-inch casserole dish.

Cook at 350° for 45 minutes.

time **saving** tips

A Special Handprint

Patty Staley

This is a wonderful project for youngsters and makes a memorable gift for mothers, grandparents, or other special people. You will need:

A piece of smooth, light-colored tile, at least 6" x 6". It needs to be wide and tall enough for a child's hand. The bigger the tile, the more embellishments you can add.

Tempera paint, your favorite color
Floral or other pretty stickers
Clear acrylic spray sealer

Paint the palm side of the child's hand.

Help the child make his or her handprint on the tile.

Let the paint dry.

Next, you can decorate with stickers.

If you like, you can use a permanent marker to write "Happy Mother's Day" or some other message.

When fully decorated, spray with the sealer and set aside till dry.

Be sure to write the date plus the child's name and age on the back.

Can be displayed on a small decorative easel or even framed.

easy **recipes**

"Creamy" Broccoli Soup

This soup gives the appearance of being creamy, although it has no cream or milk in it.

1 $\frac{1}{2}$ lbs. broccoli, stemmed and chopped
3 cups chicken broth
2 medium-sized green onions, cut in two-inch lengths
1 stalk celery, strings removed and chopped
$\frac{1}{2}$ tsp. salt

Combine all ingredients in medium saucepan.

Cover and cook over medium-low heat until broccoli is tender, about 7 minutes.

Purée in blender in batches until smooth, and serve.

Hidden Talents

Darla Satterfield Davis

There are different ways that God works through
people but the same God. God works in all of us
in everything we do. Something from the Spirit
can be seen in each person, for the common good.
—1 Corinthians 12:6,7 NCV

Alison was tiny, quiet, and as close to invisible as a child could be. She had moved eleven times before the fourth grade, and her actions towards the other children let me know she had little to no hope of forming any long-lasting friendships here either. Alison did poor work, but did not qualify for any of the myriad of special programs in our district.

Two-thirds of my class that year was composed of wild, boisterous boys. I was afraid Alison would disappear altogether in that group, so I asked God for wisdom. I felt impressed to put Alison with a group of my most outspoken boys. I made her the "captain" of the group and told her and all the other captains what I wanted them to accomplish.

Alison took her role very seriously and began to organize the boys to complete the job at hand. They laughed and joked at first, but Alison dropped her arms and stared silently at them until they complied. She never said a word; she just waited. I would not have taken her for a leader by any means, but there she was—organized, working ahead of schedule, and the boys had never been more well behaved or on task.

Alison's group presentation was far superior to any other group in the room. It was uncharacteristically neat, detailed, and showed imagination. When commenting on this in class, I asked what she attributed her great success to. She said, "You made me the captain. That means you think I am smart. No one has ever thought I was smart before, so I prayed for Jesus to make me smart."

make **your** day count

Do you have an Alison in your class? If so, ask God to give you creative ways to draw out that student's God-given gifts and talents. Assign a special task today, and voice your confidence to that student, encouraging him or her every step of the way.

Older and Wiser

Shanna D. Gregor

These older women must train the younger women.

—Titus 2:4 NLT

In addition to my natural mother, God has given me spiritual mentors—or spiritual mothers. It has proven a great help to hear the wisdom and counsel of those a little older and much wiser than I am.

One of my mother/mentors taught me that you don't always have to give children the complete answer to all of their questions, but keep the answers simple and age appropriate.

One afternoon my kindergartner asked me right out, "Mama, what is sex?" I tried to put on that brave, not-shocked-at-all face that my spiritual mother had put on when answering her teenagers' questions. I held my breath for a minute, and then a wonderful answer by the Holy Spirit came to me. Calmly I responded, "Well, that means that you're a boy or a girl. You're a boy, and I'm a girl."

"Okay," he said and climbed down from his chair at the table. It was all the answer he needed, and thankfully the Lord had provided it just in time.

Do you have mentors to whom you can turn when you have questions about your profession or spiritual matters? Are you a mentor to a teacher just starting out? Becoming a mentor to another person will keep you from getting stagnant. On the other hand, benefiting from the life experience of others may prevent you from having to learn some lessons through the school of hard knocks.

make **your** day count

If you haven't already done so, consider developing a relationship with someone who is further down the road of life than you and has walked a few miles in your shoes. Then seek out someone who could benefit from some of your hard-earned life experience. Call one of them today.

A Work in Progress

Tonya Hudson

I will praise You, for I am fearfully and wonderfully made;
Marvelous are Your works,
And that my soul knows very well.

—Psalm 139:14 NKJV

There is one student in my life with whom I am more closely acquainted than any other. This particular student requires far more of my time and focus than the rest. You could say she is "challenging". Maybe you know the type.

This is the student who often procrastinates, turning what would be very beneficial learning experiences into last-minute frenzies to meet deadlines. She is frequently caught daydreaming out the window during quiet moments, which are intended for serious study. She repeatedly fails to temper her words with patience or season them with love.

On more than one occasion, this individual has arrived to class completely unprepared for the day ahead. She must frequently comfort herself with silent reminders of her good intentions. In addition to all of this, this well-meaning young lady seldom gets to bed at a reasonable hour, causing her to be even rougher around the edges.

Occasionally I find myself doubting that I will ever accomplish much with this individual. Nonetheless, God often whispers to me how precious this child is to Him and how much He loves her. He tells me of His unflinching patience and mercy toward her and assures me that He has a marvelous plan for her life. He let's me know that He is daily crafting her into the beauty she is to become. In His own image and likeness, He is molding her. God never fails to exhort me to be patient with her, so I always return to trusting Him to finish the work He has begun.

"Who is this troubled young woman?" you may ask.

I am she. I am His work in progress.

make **your** day count

Today make a list of the many good things God has deposited within you. When tempted to condemn yourself for your failings, instead, pull out your list and rejoice in what God has done (and will do) in and through your life.

time **saving** tips

Bringing the Classroom to Life

Freshen up a room and bring new life indoors by utilizing some of these simple ideas.

 Open the window.

 Place live plants in various spots around the room.

 Adopt a classroom pet.

 Light a scented candle, or put out fresh potpourri.

 Play soft classical music in the background.

 Hang posters, piñatas, mobiles, planets, airplane models, or any other fun objects from the ceiling.

Pork Chop and Rice Dinner

Minute Rice for number of people eating

Pork chops for number of people eating

1 can cream of mushroom soup (will probably need another can if serving more than 6)

Water (according to directions on package of rice for your number of servings)

Salt and pepper to taste.

Spray baking dish or pan with non-stick spray.

Sprinkle pork chops with salt and pepper.

Pour rice into pan, then place pork chops on top.

Spread soup over the other ingredients, then pour water over all.

Cover with foil and bake at 350° for 25–30 minutes. For last 10 minutes or so, remove foil and continue baking until golden brown. May need to alter time to compensate for thicker chops.

Serve with a tossed salad, and you have a complete meal.

He'll Give You the Help You Need

Cynthia McGuire

Let us then approach the throne of grace with confidence, so that we may receive mercy and find grace to help us in our time of need.
—Hebrews 4:16

As I wake up in the morning, before the birds as most teachers do, the first thing I do is ask God to help me not to push the snooze button again! After I've gotten my coffee, I start my quiet time with God. To me this is when my day truly begins.

It's amazing, but even after an excellent night's rest, thoughts can bombard your mind in the form of distractions, worries, cares, and to-do lists. It is during this time every morning that I have to make a choice: I can choose to give way to the noise in my mind and become stressed, over-whelmed, and fatigued before the day gets underway, or I can choose to quiet my mind and seek the direction of the Lord.

Each morning I quote the Scripture above: "Let us then approach the throne of grace with confidence, so that we may receive mercy and find grace to help us in our time of need." I find that my time of need seems to be all the time, but especially first thing in the morning! But thank God His

Word says that when we need help, we can boldly go and get it! I make this Scripture personal and tell the Father that I am coming before His throne to receive the grace, mercy, and help I need for the day.

Next, I just sit in the Lord's presence and let Him fill me up, journaling anything I feel He is saying. I also read my Bible with a devotional and commit my day and myself into His hands.

The Father is available to you at all times. Go boldly to His throne to get the help you need. You won't be disappointed.

make **your** day count

Spend a few moments in God's presence and see yourself going to His throne of grace. Let Him know you need His help today, then commit the day and yourself to Him. Every time you run into a snag as you go about your business, remember, your Father is there to help you!

Get Bitter or Get Better

Lindsay Roberts

Watch out that no bitterness takes root among you,
for as it springs up it causes deep trouble,
hurting many in their spiritual lives.
—Hebrews 12:15 TLB

Throughout my miscarriages and losing my precious son after just thirty-six hours, I repeatedly had to choose whether I was going to get *bitter and be destroyed* or get *better and let God take over.* It was a decision that only I could make, and I knew that once I made the choice, there would be no turning back. If I was going to get better, I knew I had to believe in what I was doing and never let go. Otherwise, I knew that the grief, anxiety, and hurt would eat me alive.

In your trials you, too, must recognize the fine line between getting bitter and getting better. Then you must decide which way you are going to go. This is not an area where you can "straddle the fence" or change sides. Bitterness will tear you up and do permanent damage unless you make the choice to grab it and take control of it.

At one point, it hit me like a ton of bricks that God was my God no matter what happened, not just if He healed me or my children. I had to follow Isaiah 43:18–19: "Forget the former things; do not dwell on the past. See, I am doing a new thing!" So regardless of any circumstance, I had to make the decision to let go of the past, turn, and move on if I was going to experience that "new thing" that God was wanting to do.

It is by no means easy, but once you make the decision that you are not going to get bitter, you will begin to get better. It will be your day of new beginnings as it was for me.[22]

make **your** day count

Are you harboring bitterness inside about a wrong that was done to you, a disappointment you have faced? God is still God, and He wants to give you a new beginning. Give Him that bitterness today, and then get ready for the good things He will do.

time **saving** tips

Developing Rapport with Students and Their Parents

Amanda Pilgrim

The saying, "You catch more flies with honey than with vinegar," applies to the classroom, as well. Try to achieve the best possible relationship with your students and their parents. Doing so will engender optimum cooperation.

Send notes and letters:

A simple note can brighten a child's day and form a bond between teacher and student. A note can also be sent home to parents, praising their child for a job well done.

Return all calls promptly:

This will not only establish good rapport, it will be greatly appreciated.

Keep in close contact with parents before a problem arises:

Parents like to hear that their child is doing well. Don't wait until there is a problem to contact them. Capture the opportunity to say, "Thank you," "Good job," "I noticed," "I understand," or "Good point." This will build a connection between you, the student, and the parents.

Admit when you are wrong:

There is no better way to win the respect of your class than to openly and quickly admit when you are wrong.

easy **recipes**

Lindsay's Goulash[23]

Lindsay Roberts

1 ½ cups macaroni
2 lbs. extra lean ground beef or ground turkey
2 large onions, chopped
2 large cans of tomatoes
Canola oil

Cook macaroni according to package directions. Drain and set aside.

In a frying pan lightly coated with canola oil, brown the onions until they are transparent. Remove from pan and set aside.

In same frying pan, brown the ground meat until completely cooked. Drain off all fat.

Add the onions, macaroni, and canned tomatoes, juice and all.

Simmer until all ingredients are heated thoroughly.

time **saving** tips

More Ways to Develop Rapport with Your Students and Their Parents

Amanda Pilgrim

Write positive notes on graded papers:

Students value the notes that are written on their returned work. You never know, one of those papers could become a treasured possession.

Sit with students at lunch:

Although it is nice to have some time away from your class, take the opportunity to sit with students at lunch once in a while. You will build trust and confidence with them if they feel you really care.

Attend your students' extracurricular activities:

Children love to be supported in the activities in which they participate. Make a point to go to some of their after-school activities such as sporting events and music recitals.

Practice what you preach:

Children want to feel that you are being fair. Make sure that you abide by the rules you enforce with your class.

Send notes that require a parent's signature:

By having a specific place on assignments or notes where parents are to initial, you can quickly tell which parents have read the information and which ones might need a follow-up call.

Vegetable Medley Casserole

Abby Detcher

2 16-oz. bags broccoli, cauliflower, carrot combination
    (thawed)
2 cans cream of mushroom soup
8 oz. shredded Swiss cheese
1 cup sour cream
$\frac{1}{2}$ tsp. pepper
2 cans French fried onions

In a large bowl, combine veggies, soup, half the Swiss cheese,
    sour cream, pepper and 1 can of onions.

Put in a greased 9 x 13 inch pan.

Bake at 350° for 30 minutes.

Sprinkle the rest of the cheese and onions on top and bake for
    10 minutes longer.

A Wonderful Place to Be

Holly Sonnenschein

Finally, brothers, whatever is true, whatever is noble,
whatever is right, whatever is pure, whatever is lovely,
whatever is admirable—if anything is excellent or
praiseworthy—think about such things.
—Philippians 4:8

The atmosphere of the classroom is a huge thing for me as a teacher. Since we spend so much time there each day, I desire it to be a place that is as welcoming and inviting as possible, a place where people can almost sense the presence of God and the sweetness of His Spirit as they enter the room. I want it to be a positive, encouraging place that makes people glad to be there.

To accomplish this, I sprinkle the room with anything from Bible verses and quotes to pictures of God's beautiful creation. No matter where a person looks, he or she sees something beautiful, uplifting, encouraging, and faith building. To further enhance the peaceful atmosphere in our classroom, I allow the students to play instrumental and inspirational music during study and seatwork time.

Because each student is part of God's magnificent handiwork, I dedicate a large section of wall space to display a picture of each one. Next to their pictures, I allow them to put up other pictures of their own. In this corner of the classroom, we have a sofa and cozy reading area, where the students can take turns "kicking back." Sometimes I teach while sitting on the sofa with the students sitting on the floor around me to create a laid back feeling of togetherness and unity.

My goal is to make the students' entire classroom experience a wonderful one where they are exposed to things that bring life. There is nothing like welcoming the Lord into every part of your day—especially your classroom.

make **your** day count

If you haven't already done so, why not set up a special corner of the room for some "kick back and relax" time. Ask your students for their ideas about decorating the room and spend an afternoon implementing them.

God Will Vindicate You

Darla Satterfield Davis

No weapon forged against you will prevail,
and you will refute every tongue that accuses you.
This is the heritage of the servants of the Lord.
—Isaiah 54:17

Rene, an excellent teacher and friend, called in tears one evening. She had a tough teaching position in special education to start with. Now it seemed her new supervisor was gunning for her.

"I know I'm not perfect," she shared, "but I am doing the work of two teachers already, and now they have removed my part-time aide and almost doubled my paperwork. I was written up today for being two hours late turning in my lesson plans! You can't believe the scathing remarks Phyllis made on the reprimand. She made it sound like I *never* turn in my paperwork on time and that I don't comply with school policy." We ended the conversation by praying for Phyllis and asking God to resolve the issue.

The situation continued to worsen despite Rene's efforts to please her boss. Finally, she approached Phyllis and asked if she had done anything to offend her. Rene assured Phyllis that she was serious about her work and was committed to keeping an excellent track record. But the situation only worsened, and Phyllis began to publicly dress down Rene in front of staff and students.

Rene and I began to claim the promise in Isaiah 54:17, thanking God that no weapon forged against Rene would prevail. When the situation finally worsened to the point of threatening Rene's job, she called the teacher's association and asked for help.

Rene never had to say another word. The representative went in, pulled her record, and spent an hour with the superintendent. The supervisor was reassigned, Rene's record was cleared, and the aide that had been pulled was reinstated.

make **your** day count

Do you feel that you are under attack or being treated unfairly?
Take the matter to God and ask Him for wisdom in handling the situation.
Then, ask Him to intervene on your behalf, and thank Him for
His promise that no weapon forged against you will prevail.

Learning to Trust Again

Amanda Pilgrim

As for me, I trust in You, O LORD.
—Psalm 31:14 NKJV

I found Amy after school crying uncontrollably in the bathroom. When I asked her what was wrong, she blurted out the story of how her older sister, Beth, had been killed in a car accident the year before. She said she had been angry at God for a long time and that because of it, she was no longer participating in her Bible study or going to church. She wanted to know why God had let her sister die.

I pulled Amy close and, looking deep into her eyes, explained that God loved her and Beth very much and that He was also heartbroken over the loss.

"It's not that Beth sinned, but there is sin in this world, and bad things happen to good people, Amy. But know that one day we will be reunited with our loved ones in heaven. There will be no more death or tears," I soothed.

Drying her tears, Amy began to tell me about Beth and what a wonderful person she was and how active she had been in church and youth activities.

I said, "It sounds like Beth loved Jesus very much and that she lived her life for Him. What do you think she would say to you if she knew you had given up on God?"

"She would be disappointed. She'd probably tell me that I should trust God, that someday I would understand."

Eventually Amy did regain her love and trust in the Lord, and today she is very involved in her church and several outreach programs. She has even begun an outreach for young people who have lost loved ones, using her experience to console others and inspire renewed hope.

make **your** day count

Establish a relationship of trust with your students by assuring them that they can come and speak to you privately and confidentially about the things that are troubling them. Tell them today.

time **saving** tips

Engaging Students in Classroom Participation

Amanda Pilgrim

The more participation you can have out of a class, the more your students will remember about the discussion. Involving students in the learning process is a great way to guarantee the retention of the lesson.

Form "tribes":

Establish tribes by setting desks into groups. Each tribe creates its own name and team flag. Allow the tribes to work on specific assignments, and make each group responsible for the behavior of its members. Tally points on a bulletin board for each tribe with the promise of a reward for the winning group. The positive peer pressure can serve as a great incentive for improving grades and class behavior.

Allow students to participate in decision making:

Students don't mind following the rules if they feel they have had a hand in establishing them.

Vary the media in your classroom:

Students learn in a variety of ways and respond to diversity. Use that to your advantage. Different forms of media can produce better retention of the subject matter. Examples include newspapers, videos, the Internet, magazines, and special guest speakers.

Creamy Spinach Dip

1 10-oz. package frozen chopped spinach, thawed

1 ½ cups sour cream

1 cup mayonnaise

1 pkg. Knorr Vegetable Soup dry soup mix

1 8-oz. can water chestnuts, finely chopped

3 green onions, finely chopped

Put spinach in strainer and press water out till dry.

In medium bowl, stir together spinach and all other ingredients.

Cover and refrigerate for 2 hours.

Stir before serving.

Serving idea: Scoop out a round loaf of pumpernickel bread to use as a serving bowl for dip.

Help Them Find Their Spot

Holly Sonnenschein

To enjoy your work and to accept your lot in life—
that is indeed a gift from God.
—Ecclesiastes 5:19 TLB

When was it that you knew you were supposed to be a teacher? Maybe you were halfway through college before you realized it, or perhaps you have always known and never even considered doing anything else. Maybe you just had a love for kids and felt a quiet tug on your heart that teaching is what God had designed you to do. Regardless of what led you to become a teacher, it is the position that God has appointed for us. We are called! There is something special in knowing that we are walking in obedience to what the Lord has called us to do.

Just as it is important for us to find our niche, our students need to know that they fit into the whole scheme of things as well. They need to feel that they are in the right place, that their position in life is important, that they are needed. I have found that a great way to achieve this in my students is to assign jobs to them. It gives them a sense of ownership and responsibility for the overall class.

The way it is set up in my class, the students must "apply" for the jobs they are interested in. Then they must be able to explain why they want the job and why they should be chosen. The jobs last for two weeks, then we rotate. The students take such pride in their responsibilities, and they are even quick to assist one another with their tasks. I am quick to praise them for a job well done and let them know how important they are to the class.

We all have a spot in life. Let's help our students find theirs today.

make **your** day count

Discuss the various jobs that need to be done in your class, then ask for volunteers. Come up with a reward system for jobs well done.

The Power of God's Love

Lindsay Roberts

Everyone who loves has been born of God and knows God. Whoever does not love does not know God, because God is love.
—1 John 4:7,8

God *is* love, and everyone who knows Him knows love. That means the words *God* and *love* are synonymous. Once I heard a minister I know, Kenneth Copeland, say that every time you see the word *God* in Scripture, you can replace it with the word *love* and vice versa.

Take 1 John 4:18, for example, which says, "Perfect love drives out fear." You could exchange the word *love* for *God*, and then it would say, "God drives out fear."

If God is the highest power of all powers and it takes His love to get rid of fear, think about how powerful fear can be. Then it's easy to see how it imprisons people—even your students. But the love of God is more powerful than anything. It can calm any situation and bring peace and hope instead.

Some people think that love is all about hearts and flowers. But getting through the tough situations in life takes more than a box of candy and a greeting card!

God's love is powerful! When you understand the power of love and ask God to pour it out through you to your students and others, you can become a bridge over troubled waters. Regardless of what you and your students face today, I encourage you to pull out your secret weapon of love.[24]

make **your** day count

Purpose in your heart today to allow God's love to flush out any fear you are dealing with and then flow through you to your students. Most people deal with fear on some level, so by loving your students with God's love, you can make a significant impact on them.

About the Author

Lindsay Roberts and her husband, Richard, were married in 1980. She began traveling with her husband, ministering throughout the world and supporting him in what the Lord has called him to do.

"After the birth of our son, Richard Oral," Lindsay says, "we were devastated when he lived only 36 hours. But God picked us up, dried our tears, and helped us try again." Out of that experience from pain to victory, Lindsay wrote *36 Hours with an Angel*—the story of how God sustained their faith after Richard Oral's death and blessed her and Richard with the miracle births of their three daughters: Jordan, Olivia, and Chloe.

Lindsay hosts *Make Your Day Count*, a daily television program full of ministry, cooking, creative tips, and lots of fun. With her husband, Richard, she also co-hosts the nightly television program *The Hour of Healing*.

Lindsay has co-authored several books, such as *A Cry for Miracles* and *Dear God, I Love to Eat, But I Sure Do Hate to Cook* cookbook. She has also written several children's books, including *ABC's of Faith for Children* and *God's Champions*.

Lindsay serves as editor of *Make Your Day Count*, a quarterly magazine aimed at today's woman; *Miracles Now*, a quarterly magazine for ministry partners; and *Your Daily Guide to Miracles*, a daily devotional book published semi-annually.

She is also a member of the Oral Roberts University Board of Regents.

"I am dedicated to God and willing to do whatever He calls me to do," Lindsay says. "I also stand in support of the call of God upon my husband. He and I are both grateful that God is using us for His glory."

Royalties from the sale of this book and others
in the *Make Your Day Count* series will go towards
the Make Your Day Count Scholarship Fund.

To contact Lindsay Roberts
or request a free issue of the
Make Your Day Count magazine,
please write to:

Lindsay Roberts
c/o Oral Roberts Ministries
Tulsa, Oklahoma 74171-0001
or
e-mail her at:
Lindsay@orm.cc

Please visit the *Make Your Day Count* Web site at
www.makeyourdaycount.com.

*Please include your prayer requests
and comments when you write.*

If you would like to have someone join in agreement with you
in prayer as a point of contact, consider calling the Abundant Life
Prayer Group at 918-495-7777. They are there to pray with you
twenty-four hours a day, seven days a week.

About the Contributors

Nancy C. Anderson loves to speak and write to women and teens. She encourages them to replace their fears with faith and discover the freedom of an abundant life. Nancy has been a contributing author to numerous books including *God's Way for Women, God's Way for Teens, Beauty Is Soul Deep, Stuff a Girl's Gotta Know,* and *A Special Kind of Love.* Please visit her Web site at www.NancyCAnderson.com.

Emily Biffle is a kindergarten teacher at Victory Christian School in Tulsa, Oklahoma. She is a graduate of Northeastern State University in Tahlequah, Oklahoma, and is currently attending graduate school at Oral Roberts University in special education. Emily volunteers with the junior-high youth group at her church, Victory Christian Center, as well as with the Victory by Virtue class for teen girls. Victory by Virtue teaches young women about purity, holiness, and the destiny for their lives. They also have a fashion show, demonstrating modest dressing for Christian girls.

Linda Burritt has been a fifth-grade teacher at Victory Christian School in Tulsa, Oklahoma, for eight years. She has taught in both public and private schools for over twenty years and is now working on her doctorate at Oral Roberts University. Linda and her husband, Duane, have two married sons whose families also live in the Tulsa area.

Darla Satterfield Davis graduated with a bachelor of science degree in education with a minor in English. She has taught in a public school for over fifteen years and is currently an art specialist for an elementary and intermediate school. Ms. Davis is also the owner and steward of The Christian Fine Arts Center in Cleburne, Texas, which houses "Higher Grounds" Coffee House (with open mic. for Christian poets and song writers), Club City Lights (a Christian music venue with concerts every Friday and Saturday night), as well as offering classes in art, music, sign language, and drama. The Christian Fine Arts Center exists to teach people of all ages to discover and use the talents and gifts God has blessed them with and provides a safe, positive environment for these individuals to share and enjoy the presentation of their gifts. Ms. Davis is available for inspirational and motivational speaking engagements during the summer months and may be contacted at www.ChristianFineArtsCenter.com.

Abby Detcher attended Oral Roberts University in the Music department in 1986 and is a 1989 graduate of Rhema Bible Training Center in Tulsa, Oklahoma. Living in her home state of Ohio since 1992, Abby has served in numerous volunteer and paid positions in her local church. In 1996, Abby left the work force to become a full-time mother and to teach piano and music lessons, which she still enjoys. Abby, her husband, Bill, and their three children reside in Indian Springs, Ohio, where they are active in their church, Courts of Praise Christian Center.

Jackie Farell graduated from Oral Roberts University in 1983 with a bachelor's degree in science and in 1985 with a master's degree in bio-medical science. Off and on for ten years, she and her husband, Mike (also an ORU graduate), served on the mission field in southeast Asia where they smuggled Bibles into China, helped lead crusades, and produced a twelve-part discipleship-training video series in the Indonesian language. At one point Jackie substitute taught at the International School in Jakarta, Indonesia. Currently, Jackie and Mike reside in Tulsa, Oklahoma, where they are raising their eleven children whom Jackie homeschools.

Shanna D. Gregor is a wife, mother, freelance writer, and development editor.

Karen Hardin is a seasoned missionary who—along with her husband, Kevin, and their three children—has ministered in Asia for the past fifteen years. Seven of those years were spent living in China where she and Kevin taught English as a second language to university students. Karen and her husband are both alumni of Oral Roberts University and are members of the ORU Ministers Alliance. Also a freelance writer, Karen is the author of *Seasons of Life: Reflections to Celebrate the Heart of a Woman.* In addition, her work has appeared in *USA Today, Stories for the Spirit-Filled Believer, Blood and Thunder,* and *Charisma* magazine. You can contact Karen at: chcall@gorilla.net.

Dana Hicks is a kindergarten teacher at Victory Christian School in Tulsa, Oklahoma. She was raised in the Oklahoma panhandle and grew up in a small farming community where she graduated from Keyes High School. Dana earned a bachelor's degree in education in Weatherford, Oklahoma, at Southwestern Oklahoma State University. She is married and a mother of two wonderful boys who attend Victory Christian School. She is currently enrolled in master's level courses in special education at Oral Roberts University.

Tonya Hudson is a home-schooling mother of three. She and her husband, Ron, are ministry leaders at their church, Victory Christian Center in Tulsa, Oklahoma, as well as members of the church's advisory board. Tonya leads a ladies' support group through Victory's cell-group ministry and is presently pursuing a writing career. She especially enjoys writing for children. Tonya can be reached by e-mail at tonya@bbgs.us.

Linda Jordan has taught in both public and Christian schools for forty-one years, thirty-nine of those as a first-grade teacher. A graduate of Northeastern State University in Oklahoma, Linda feels that first grade is a critical year for children in that it lays the foundation for their entire education. Linda and her husband, David, are the parents of two married children and the grandparents of six grandchildren, all of whom live in the Tulsa, Oklahoma, area.

Cleo Justus has a rich diversity of experience as a pastor's wife, mother, devotional speaker, author, volunteer, and yes, a clown! Retired from her position as assistant manager of a credit union, she is now free to devote her energies to a love for writing, speaking engagements, and volunteering her time. Having earned several awards for her writings, she is also published in numerous venues with Honor Books, RiverOak Publishing, and White Stone Books. In 2001, Cleo was awarded the Senior Storyteller of the Year Award by the board of education in the city where she resides. Her latest work is a story-time tape series entitled *Bits and Pieces,* narrating true stories from her youth. Currently she ministers locally and abroad with various clown troop ministries. You may contact Cleo at: justtulip@juno.com.

Kim Lutherbeck, originally from Meridian, Mississippi, graduated from William Carey College with a bachelor of arts degree in elementary education. She received her master's degree from Oral Roberts' University in early childhood education. She has taught for six years, five of which have been at Victory Christian School in Tulsa, Oklahoma, where she now teaches K-4. Kim and her husband, Kevin, are involved in their church, Victory Christian Center, where they currently help in the leadership of the singles' ministry.

Cynthia McGuire graduated from Oral Roberts University in 1996 with a degree in elementary education and has been teaching at Victory Christian School in Tulsa, Oklahoma, for eight years. In 2003, Cynthia received the honor of Teacher of the Year; in 2000, she was named Honorary Teacher of the Year; and in 1996, she was named Rookie of the Year. She has been a guest with her sisters on the *Make Your Day Count* television broadcast as well as *Something Good Tonight,* which is hosted by her pastors Billy Joe and Sharon Daugherty of Victory Christian Center. Cynthia's hobbies include traveling, shopping, exercise, and quiet time with God; and her passions are children, walking in the will of God daily, and always being an encourager.

Stephanie Carlile Murrill graduated from Union College in Lincoln, Nebraska, and is the fourth- through sixth-grade teacher at Tulsa Adventist Academy in Tulsa, Oklahoma. She enjoys writing stories about her experiences in the classroom as a new teacher and is currently planning her May 2004 wedding to Mark Murrill. Stephanie can be contacted at sjcarlile@yahoo.com.

Janet A. Nation and her husband, Galen, have served on the staff of two churches where they have taught numerous classes on marriage-related topics, conducted marriage retreats, and counseled couples in troubled marriages. From 1997–1999, they lived in Wuhan, China; and from 2002–2003, they lived in Xuzhou, China. In both instances they moved to China to teach university students, Janet teaching English as a second language and Galen teaching engineering courses. They are the parents of three grown children—two of whom are graduates of Oral Roberts University—and have three grandchildren. Janet and Galen currently reside in Tulsa, Oklahoma.

Georgia Lee Paul is a fifth-grade teacher at Victory Christian School in Tulsa, Oklahoma. She earned her undergraduate degree in elementary education in 1999 from Oral Roberts University, and she will graduate again from ORU in 2004 with a masters in public school administration. Missions is her passion, and she has been to over twenty countries, most recently St. Petersburg, Russia, where she worked with children in summer camps.

Amanda Pilgrim, Managing Editor for White Stone Books, resides in Tulsa, Oklahoma, with her husband, Mike, and their many animals. She is a former junior high and high school teacher and has been a coach for the Little Dribblers basketball league, along with junior varsity and varsity girls' basketball. Amanda enjoys writing about her experiences as a teacher and coach and can be contacted at gsupreme@cox.net.

Evelyn Roberts, wife of Evangelist Oral Roberts, has been by his side in the ministry for over fifty years. Mrs. Roberts is Lindsay Roberts' mother-in-law. She is the author of several books and is a Lifetime Spiritual Regent on the Oral Roberts University Board of Regents. She is also a member of the International Charismatic Bible Ministries Board of Trustees and has been a speaker at the Lindsay Roberts Women's Conferences. Mrs. Roberts attended Northeastern State University in Oklahoma and Texas College of Arts and Industries in Kingville, Texas, and taught school three years before marrying Oral. They are the parents of four children; thirteen grandchildren, one of whom is in heaven; and three great-grandchildren. For more information, visit www.orm.cc.

Cindy Schaefer is a freelance writer and photographer who lives in Stillwater, Oklahoma. She and her husband, Scott, have been in youth ministry for the past five years.

Holly Sonnenschein taught fourth grade at Victory Christian School in Tulsa, Oklahoma, from 2001–2003. Prior to that, she taught third grade in Carrolton, Texas, as well as overseas for a few weeks in Romania. Holly's heartbeat is to make an impact on kids' lives and to pour God's love on them like crazy!

Patty Staley has taught in public schools for six years and is now at Victory Christian School in Tulsa, Oklahoma, where she has taught for twenty years. She is currently the teacher of the fast-track kindergarten class, and she loves to read and go on missions trips. Patty has a passion to pass on to the next generation a love for God and hopes to someday mentor young teachers and encourage young women to seek God with all their hearts. She and her husband of twenty-six years, Ken, are the proud parents of two miracle children—Rebekah, nineteen; and Michael, fourteen.

June Anne Wakley graduated from Evangel University in Springfield, Missouri, where she played basketball and majored in early childhood and elementary education. Wanting to do away with the idea that school had to be boring and always quiet in order for children to learn, she had a lifelong dream of becoming a teacher and has taught kindergarten for six years at Victory Christian School in Tulsa, Oklahoma. June Anne and her husband, Ryan, have three children.

Endnotes

1 Lindsay Roberts, *Make Your Day Count* magazine (Tulsa, OK: Oral Roberts Evangelistic Association, April–June 2003) p. 4.

2 Lindsay Roberts, *Dear God, I Love to Eat...But I Sure Do Hate to Cook!* (Tulsa, OK: Lindsay Roberts, 2001) p. 93.

3 *American Heritage Dictionary of the English Language, New College Edition,* (Boston: Houghton Mifflin Company, 1976) p. 1085, s.v. "react"; emphasis mine.

4 Ibid., p. 1108, s.v. "respond."

5 Dori Byron, <http://www.skl.com/~guidezon/jbice.htm> (accessed Nov. 2003).

6 Lindsay Roberts, *Make Your Day Count* magazine (Oct.–Dec. 2002) p. 6.

7 Jeremiah 29:11; Matthew 10:30; Psalm 147:4.

8 Lindsay Roberts, *Richard & Lindsay Roberts Family Cookbook* (Tulsa, OK: Oral Roberts Evangelistic Association, 1990) p. 10.

9 Lindsay Roberts, *A Cry for Miracles* (Tulsa, OK: Lindsay Roberts, 1996) pp. 124–126.

10 Lindsay Roberts, *Make Your Day Count* magazine (April–June 2001) pp. 9–12.

11 Lindsay Roberts, *Make Your Day Count* magazine (Tulsa, OK: Oral Roberts Evangelistic Association, Oct.-Dec. 2001) p. 8.

12 Lindsay Roberts, *"Dear God, I love to eat...But I sure do hate to cook!"* cookbook (Tulsa, OK: Lindsay Roberts, 2001) p. 6.

13 Lindsay Roberts, *Make Your Day Count* magazine (Oct.–Dec. 2001) p. 7.

14 *"Dear God, I love to eat...But I sure do hate to cook!"* cookbook, p. 8.

15 *"Dear God, I love to eat...But I sure do hate to cook!"* cookbook, p. 20.

16 *"Dear God, I love to eat...But I sure do hate to cook!"* cookbook, p. 49.

17 Lindsay Roberts, *Miracles Now* (July–Sept. 2003) pp. 10–11.

18 Lindsay Roberts, *Make Your Day Count* magazine (Jan.–March 2002) pp. 7–8.

19 *"Dear God, I love to eat...But I sure do hate to cook!"* cookbook, p. 64.

20 Lindsay Roberts, *Miracles Now* (Nov.–Dec. 2000) pp. 14–15.

21 Lindsay Roberts, *Stress Less Living* (Tulsa, OK: Harrison House Publishers, 2003) pp. 4–7.

22 Lindsay Roberts, *36 Hours with an Angel* (Tulsa, OK: Oral Roberts Evangelistic Association, Inc., 1990) pp. 121–122, 126.

23 Lindsay Roberts, *Richard & Lindsay Roberts Family Cookbook,* p. 113.

24 Lindsay Roberts, *Make Your Day Count* magazine (Tulsa, OK: Oral Roberts Evangelistic Association, Oct.–Dec. 2002) pp. 6–7.

Prayer of Salvation

God loves you—no matter who you are, no matter what your past. God loves you so much that He gave His one and only begotten Son for you. The Bible tells us that "whoever believes in him shall not perish but have eternal life" (John 3:16). Jesus laid down His life and rose again so that we could spend eternity with Him in heaven and experience His absolute best on earth. If you would like to receive Jesus into your life, say the following prayer out loud and mean it from your heart:

> *Heavenly Father, I come to You, admitting that I am a sinner. Right now, I choose to turn away from sin, and I ask You to cleanse me of all unrighteousness. I believe that Your Son, Jesus, died on the cross to take away my sins. I also believe that He rose again from the dead so that I might be forgiven of my sins and made righteous through faith in Him. I call upon the name of Jesus Christ to be the Savior and Lord of my life. Jesus, I choose to follow You and ask that You fill me with the power of the Holy Spirit. I declare that right now I am a child of God. I am free from sin and full of the righteousness of God. I am saved in Jesus' name. Amen.*

If you prayed this prayer to receive Jesus Christ as your Lord and Savior for the first time, please contact us on the Web at **www.harrisonhouse.com** to receive a free book.

Or you may write to us at:

Harrison House
P.O. Box 35035
Tulsa, Oklahoma 74153

Other Books in the
Make Your Day Count Devotional Series

Make Your Day Count Devotional for Women
Make Your Day Count Devotional for Teens
Make Your Day Count Devotional for Mothers

Additional copies of this book
are available from your local bookstore.

If this book has been a blessing to you
or if you would like to see more of the
Harrison House product line,
please visit us on our Web site at
www.harrisonhouse.com.

HARRISON HOUSE
Tulsa, Oklahoma 74153

The Harrison House Vision

Proclaiming the truth and the power

Of the Gospel of Jesus Christ

With excellence;

Challenging Christians to

Live victoriously,

Grow spiritually,

Know God intimately.